25 Years of TALLADEGA Superspeedway

A QUARTER-CENTURY OF RACING

at the

WORLD'S GREATEST SPEEDWAY

By Clyde Bolton

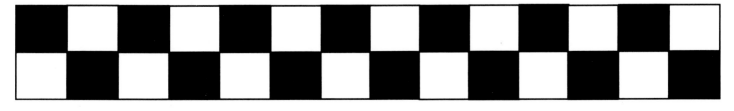

FOR LAUREN...

ABOUT THE AUTHOR

Clyde Bolton, a sports columnist with *The Birmingham News*, broke the story that Talladega Superspeedway would be built, and he has covered racing at the track since it opened in 1969. He has won numerous national awards for his writing, including the 1985 American Motor Sports Award of Excellence for the best story in the United States on Winston Cup racing. He is the author of four novels and nine non-fiction books, including *Remembering Davey*, a biography of the late Davey Allison, and *Bolton's Best Stories of Auto Racing*, a collection of his newspaper columns and stories. Bolton and his wife, Sandra, live in Trussville, AL.

ACKNOWLEDGEMENTS

UMI Publications, Inc. is proud to bring you Talladega's 25th Anniversary book. Clyde Bolton put in many long hours to bring you the story of every NASCAR Winston Cup event, Clyde knows as much about Talladega as anyone. The photos in this book are the work of Bob Mauk & John Mauk from NASCAR Archives along with Mr. Bob Castanzo, David Chobat and James Roy. All of these folks poured over and through their files to bring you this race action.

We would like to extend extra special thanks to Mr. Grant Lynch and Mr. Jim Freeman. Without their help, guidance, and patience, none of this would have been possible.

This book is for you, the NASCAR FAN. Please enjoy.

TALLADEGA SUPERSPEEDWAY TRACK OFFICIALS
PRESIDENT-Grant Lynch
PUBLIC RELATIONS DIRECTOR-Jim Freeman, DIRECTOR OF HOSPITALITY-Jana Butts, MANAGER OF
PROMOTIONS AND OPERATIONS-Scott Duncan, TRACK SUPERINTENDENT-Larry Johnson
DIRECTOR OF TICKETING-Larry Allen

Talladega 25th Anniversary Staff: Publisher-Ivan Mothershead, Associate Publisher-Charlie Keiger, Associate Publisher-Merry Schoonmaker, Senior Editor-Amy Vail, Assistant Editors-Mark Cantey, Jeff Huneycutt, Terry McCorkle and Jason Simon, Layout and Design-Brett Shippy and Michael McBride

TABLE OF CONTENTS

FOREWORD

Talladega Superspeedway is 25 years old this year, and the first quarter of a century has produced some of the most memorable racing in motorsports history. When Bill France Sr. had the track built in 1968-69, its length and design guaranteed that it would open as the world's fastest speedway. In the 25 years since, it has also earned the reputation as one of the most competitive.

Typical Talladega finishes finds three, four, five and even ten cars battling for the checkered flag. Two of the more memorable finishes were the 1981 Talladega 500, when Ron Bouchard literally nosed out Darrell Waltrip and Terry Labonte, and last year's DieHard 500, when Dale Earnhardt prevailed over Ernie Irvin by the width of a bumper.

This book, written by renowned motorsports journalist Clyde Bolton, captures all of these memories in a very personal style that makes this book "must" reading for racing fans everywhere. Clyde has gone behind the scenes and talked to the folks that made things happen.

Get in your easy chair, buckle in, and get ready to enjoy 25 years of motorsports reading at its very best.

Bill France Jr.

Bill France Jr., (left) speaks with his father, Bill France Sr.,(right) whom he succeeded as head of NASCAR in 1972.

If a man had accepted a 15-cent collect call, the property that Talladega Superspeedway occupies might be planted in soybeans. Stock car racing might consist merely of amateurs dueling in battered hotrods on dirt tracks before small crowds.

And William Henry Getty "Big Bill" France might have spent his life pumping gasoline and changing oil at his filling station.

Instead, the world's largest, fastest speedway dominates a span of the Alabama countryside known as Dry Valley. Stock car competition outdraws Indianapolis-type racing, and France, who died in 1992 at age 82, is remembered as its key figure.

It is doubtful any other individual in the history of American sports was as important to his game as France, the builder of Talladega Superspeedway, was to stock car racing.

France was born in Washington, D.C., and as a teenager would play hooky and go to the 1 1/8-mile board track at Laurel, MD, and marvel as the Dusenbergs screamed by.

He even managed to slip the family car onto the track for a few laps. "Dad didn't know it, of course," France once said. "The toughest part later was keeping a straight face when he went down to the tire dealer to complain about the tires wearing out so fast on the Model T."

France quit high school after two years and went to work in a garage. He built a wooden car that was covered with canvas, and when he drove the contraption in competition on a half-mile track in Pikeville, MD, he officially became a race driver. In later years he marveled that it didn't catch fire.

He worked at a service station, and one of his jobs was responding to calls from customers whose cars wouldn't start on bitter cold mornings. He was the one who had to get them rolling.

"I decided that if I was going to have to fix automobiles for a living, I might as well fix them where it wasn't snowing," France said. "I decided I might as well do it in Florida."

"I saw Daytona Beach and thought it was the prettiest place I'd ever seen," he said. "I still do."

Legend has it that France's car broke down there, the family was stranded, and the course of history was thus diverted. "That's not true," he said. "I was a mechanic, so I would have fixed the car. We stayed in Daytona because we liked it."

Daytona, with its flat, hard beach, had been a center of timed speed runs since 1902. France himself saw Sir Malcolm Campbell set a record of 276 miles an hour in 1935 in the Bluebird, which is now on display at the International Motorsports' Hall of Fame museum next door to Talladega Superspeedway.

But timed runs moved to the more spacious, safer Bonneville Salt Flats in Utah, and Daytona sought a new attraction. It decided on a stock car race on a makeshift course that employed the beach as one straightaway and a parallel highway as the other with horseshoe turns connecting the two. The city would promote the event.

France drove in the first beach-road race in 1936. He finished fifth, but he was the mechanic on the winning car.

The city lost money and bade race promotion farewell. The Elks Club promoted the second race, but its venture sank in red ink, too.

France was a race driver, and his service station on Main Street was a gathering place for others. The chamber of commerce naturally asked him if he knew of anyone who might promote a beach-road race.

This is where the 15-cent collect call came in. France tried to contact a promoter who lived in Orange City, but the man refused his call. So France and Charlie Reese, a restaurant owner who also owned the racer France drove, said what the heck, they'd do it themselves. France had no money, but he would do the work and Reese would put up the cash.

Thus France's career as a race promoter was born. He made money on the beach-road events and began putting on shows at other tracks.

Stock car racing was haphazard and held in low esteem during France's early days of promoting. Many promoters were crooks. France remembered one announcing he would pay $500 to the winner but giving the victor only $50. "That figure was just to impress the public," the promoter explained. Others skipped out with the gate receipts before the race ended.

France believed that if it were given a strong framework, stock car racing would prosper. So, in 1947, he organized the National Association for Stock Car Auto Racing. NASCAR would have uniform rules and an insurance plan, and it would guarantee the purse.

It also would award points at each race and recognize each season's champion. "The American people want statistics," France said. "That's why they remember O.J.

"It is doubtful any other individual in the history of American sports was as important to his game as France was to stock car racing."

Simpson and Pete Rose. They want to know about champions, how much money they won, the records they established."

The first NASCAR-sanctioned race was held on Feb. 15, 1948, on the beach-road course. It was for modified cars, and Red Byron of Atlanta, formerly of Anniston, AL, which is near Talladega, won it.

Stock car racing meant hotrods, usually tiny coupes with souped-up engines. That was the combination that would go fastest, so that was what should be raced, everyone reasoned.

But part of France's genius lay in his belief that fans would turn out to see new sedans that looked like the ones they drove to work. He thought a man who drove, for instance, a Ford every day would have a rooting interest in a Ford at speed.

So, in 1949, NASCAR ran its first event in what France would shortly thereafter christen the Grand National series. It was contested on a dirt track in Charlotte. Late model competition quickly became so popular that it replaced modified racing as NASCAR's marquee attraction.

(The premier series of NASCAR racing is now called Winston Cup. Today, Grand National designates another circuit, different from the original Grand National. For purposes of clarity, the name Winston Cup is used throughout this book when referring to the main series, except when quoting directly.)

France knew that stock car racing could flourish only if better facilities were built. The answer to the need came when Harold Brasington constructed Darlington Raceway—the first in a chain of Southern superspeedways—and in 1950, the initial Southern 500 was run under NASCAR sanction. NASCAR and Darlington complemented each other, and each prospered.

France himself built Dixie's second superspeedway. His 2.5-mile Daytona International Speedway hosted the first Daytona 500 in 1959, and that facility truly lifted stock car racing into the big leagues. It was the same size as Indianapolis Motor Speedway—which for decades had been synonymous with racing in the U.S.—but it was superior in design to Indy what with its high banks and dogleg in the front stretch "so the fans weren't looking into their next-door neighbor's ear all the time."

France once was ushered out of the pits at mighty Indy, and he never forgot it. "They resented the president of a rival association being in their pits," he said.

"We were trying to figure out a way to build the

Daytona track before—but then we really went to it in earnest."

France wasn't finished when he completed his Daytona track that an Indianapolis newspaper had labeled a "pipe dream speedway." He built another course, one even larger than Daytona's. The 2.66-mile Alabama International Motor Speedway opened in 1969. Sleepy Dry Valley had itself the biggest, fastest, most competitive, most unpredictable race track in the world.

Later, the International Speedway Corp.(which owns Daytona and Talladega) would acquire Darlington, the original Southern superspeedway, and operate the famed road course at Watkins Glen.

Another dream of France's that materialized was the International Motorsports Hall of Fame adjacent to Talladega Superspeedway. When 150 members of the worldwide motorsports press voted the first class of inductees into the hall of fame in 1990, Bill France's name led all the rest.

France built his empire by being as tough as whit leather. For years he was a one-man show. Things weren't done by committee. There is a story, probably apocryphal, that his son, Bill France Jr., glanced over a reporter's shoulder and saw that the man was writing that his pop was a dictator. "Why don't you make that benevolent dictator?" he is supposed to have suggested.

France's wife Anne worked by his side. She was an officer in NASCAR and the speedway corporation before her death in 1992.

In 1972, France retired as president of NASCAR and handed the reins to Bill Jr. In 1981, he stepped aside as president of the speedway corporation—remaining as chairman of the board—and Bill Jr. assumed that post. Today Bill Jr. is president of NASCAR and chairman of the board and CEO of International Speedway Corp., and Jim France, his brother, is executive vice president and secretary of NASCAR and president and assistant treasurer of ISC.

Just as Big Bill was the right man to take stock car racing by the nape of the neck and shake it into respectability, Bill Jr. has been the right man to run it during the years of continued growth. He is regarded as an immensely competent sports executive.

Naturally, he grew up with the sound of a racing engine in one ear and the sound of an adding machine in the other.

William Clifton France (technically he is not a junior, but he was called Bill Jr. early on, and it stuck) made his management debut at that first NASCAR late model race in 1949. "I pulled guys off the fence who tried to slip in," he recalled. "I was about 13. No, it wasn't too dangerous. They were interested in seeing a race, not in whipping me."

"He was a little young for a bouncer," his father said, "but he was pretty stout."

That wasn't Bill Jr.'s only job at that historic race. "I parked cars and cleaned up and did the bumper stripping. That was a form of advertising. We did a lot of outdoor advertising. We didn't have enough money to buy ads in the papers, and we couldn't get anything run in the sports pages. We had to buy signs and nail them to sides of tobacco barns."

Bill France Jr. knew that he was destined to some day run NASCAR—but, like any other kid who ever went to the speedway, he wanted to run a race car.

"That was where the glamour was, in driving," he said. "Ask any youngster whether he goes to the track to see a NASCAR official or a race driver," Bill Jr. suggested. "I was no different."

So his father put him in a Grand National car and turned him loose.

"One night in Greensboro I parked cars outside the track until the public address announcer said it was time to start the race. Then I put on my helmet and ran to my race car.

"I couldn't even compete in the next Grand National race because we had a modified race somewhere, and I had to work there. It was then I realized that if you were going to go racing, you had to go racing. So I quit.

"Yeah, I used to wonder how good I could have been, but that's all history. I never even think about it now."

The boss of Talladega Superspeedway learned every aspect of racing by doing it. He has flagged races, been chief steward, sold soft drinks, programs and tickets. He has crashed a stock car.

He even met his wife, Betty Jane, through racing. The future Mrs. Bill France Jr. attended a race at Bowman-Gray Stadium in Winston-Salem, NC. Although she wasn't in the race, she won - NASCAR's future president.

> *"France built his NASCAR empire by being as tough as whit leather. For years he was a one-man show."*

Grant Lynch, Talladega Superspeedway President.

"Talladega Superspeedway already is the most competitive track in Winston Cup racing," said Grant Lynch, the president, "and our goal is to make it the most fan-friendly place on the circuit."

Crowds were continuing to increase, he pointed out, "and we are planning on making the speedway a better place to spend the day. I think you'll see more tower grandstands, and service facilities for customers will continue to be improved. There will be more concession stands, more restrooms, more campground space, all the amenities."

Lynch, in February of 1993, became the third general manager in the history of the speedway. Don Naman was the first and Mike Helton the second. Lynch was promoted to president in November of 1993, succeeding Helton.

"I just want to continue to build upon what Don and Mike did to make the speedway one of the premier places for motorsports in America," said Lynch.

Lynch came to Talladega after 10 years of representing the interests of R.J. Reynolds Sports Marketing.

Lynch is a family man (he and his wife Marcia have two young daughters, Ashley and Sara Katherine) and an outdoorsman, a fellow who played the rough game of rugby in college.

"I think I'm a fun person," he said. "I think you're going to get a lot more done with a jar of honey than with a bottle of vinegar. I'm serious about what I do, but I like to have a laugh and a smile when I do it."

Lynch played rugby for North Carolina State and Wake Forest—though he wasn't really enrolled at Wake Forest. "It was a club sport," he explained with a chuckle. "I was featured in their annual for two years and wasn't even a student."

Later, he started up a rugby team in Winston-Salem, NC, where he lived. "You spend 80 minutes pounding a guy, and then you spend two hours with him having a beer and talking about when you are going to do it again," he said.

"It's a great sport. I got a separated shoulder and a broken collarbone and had knee surgery from it, but I'd do it again."

Lynch became acquainted with all the NASCAR speedways when he worked in stock car racing for R.J. Reynolds.

"Winston Cup racing is probably the best and highest quality racing in the U.S." he said. "That's a direct result of NASCAR's efforts to make it so. I don't think it's because of technological development so much as because of NASCAR's stewardship, being sure everybody is playing on a level field. That's what keeps the fans coming to the stands."

Lynch, 39, sees himself as "a big outdoorsman. I love hunting and fishing. That's one of the things that enticed me to come to Alabama. There's a quality of life that you can have here that you might not have in a lot of other states.

"When I was in North Carolina, if you had asked me to pick five states where I'd like to live, Alabama would have been one of them."

Naman, now executive director of the International Motorsports Hall of Fame which is located next door to Talladega Superspeedway, is from Brooklyn, NY, and he never saw a stock car race until 1960. He joined the Air

Sr.'s draft. Nobody will ever pass him. When I have to face a problem, I ask myself, 'What would Bill France Sr. do?"

Helton succeeded Naman and eventually was named president of Talladega Superspeedway. He left to become NASCAR's vice- president of competition in November of 1993.

"I was raised in Bristol," Helton said. "It's hard to be raised in Bristol and not be exposed to racing, because of the track that is there."

Force, and his tour included Knoxville, TN; while living there, a friend took him to the Atlanta 500. "By the time that day was over, I knew I wanted to be associated with NASCAR racing," he said.

"Winston Cup racing is probably the best and highest quality racing in the U.S. That's a direct result of NASCAR's efforts to make it so."

After high school and while he was in college, Helton began driving on the dirt tracks. He continued to race regularly for four or five years. "I finally woke up and realized I wasn't the greatest driver in the world," he said, "and I'd better find some other way to hang around the tracks."

He became a drag racer and won more than 200 races. Later, he was the promoter at a short track in Maryville, TN, and its success led the France family to name him general manager at Talladega in 1970.

The speedway experienced dramatic growth under Naman as he added thousands of seats, built a roof over many seats, expanded the camping, parking, and garage areas and built service buildings. Crowds increased from the 30,000s to the 130,000s under him.

"There has been a steady growth through my time, Mike Helton's and Grant Lynch's," said Naman. "That's been the philosophy, to grow steadily and put proceeds back into the facility."

In 1988 he resigned and took over the hall of fame which, like the speedway, was one of Big Bill France's dreams.

"I left the speedway because I felt I had reached the goal I set of sellout crowds and the track becoming known worldwide," he said. "I had been asked three times to go to the hall of fame, and the fourth time I did.

"I've tried throughout my career to ride in Bill France

He began doing odd jobs at Bristol International, and that led to his being named publicity director at Atlanta International. When he left Atlanta in 1985 he had risen to the rank of general manager. He was director of promotion and marketing development at Daytona International before coming to Talladega.

The track continued to develop under Helton; thousands of seats and numerous buildings were added. When the speedway opened, seating was in the 50,000 range. At the end of his tenure it was about 82,000.

Talladega Superspeedway and Winston Cup racing have grown but, as Helton pointed out nostalgically, "The good old boy era is slipping away."

The first race he can remember seeing was the Volunteer 500 at Bristol in 1965. "My dad couldn't afford tickets, so we parked on a farmer's hillside," he said. "We could see about a third of the track.

"I remember being amazed that Ned Jarrett won the race in a Ford Galaxie just like the one my daddy drove."

On Sept. 4, 1966, *The Birmingham News* broke a story that said: "A six-million-dollar automobile race track the same length as those at Indianapolis and Daytona appears to be a virtual certainty for the Birmingham area."

The story quoted William H.G. France, president of NASCAR and "spokesman for a group interested in building the facility" as saying that, in his opinion, the track would be constructed.

Others voiced optimism. "I feel sure we're going to build it," Dr. James L. Hardwick, mayor of Talladega, said.

"I think we're going to get it if we work at it hard enough and long enough," O.V. Hill, chairman of the Talladega Industrial Development Board, said.

France spoke guardedly about the track, citing a tight money market as a problem and cautioning, "We worked on Daytona seven years before we ever broke ground." He would not say unequivocally that a speedway would be constructed.

But on Oct. 17, 1966, at a joint meeting of Talladega civic clubs, France announced that a track would indeed be built some 45 miles from Birmingham. The property would include some land used by Talladega's old airport and some adjacent to it. The speedway would be 2.5 miles in length, same as the one in Daytona, and cars would travel about the same speed as at Daytona. This track, though, would be a quad-oval, "sort of a rounded diamond," whereas Daytona's was a tri-oval.

France said he hoped ground could be broken in the spring or summer of 1967 with the first race in the spring of 1969. The working name of the track: Alabama International Motor Sports and Testing Facility at Talladega.

Stock car racing had many followers in the football-crazy area, but for many others it was still an arcane sport. It wasn't on television every weekend as it is now. There were a couple of racing Allison brothers in Hueytown whose names seemed to be in the papers a lot, and there was a track outside Atlanta that seemed to host big races, but for thousands, stock car racing conjured up a vague image of jalopies kicking up dirt and making too much noise.

"I thought it was crazy to use that good old soybean land to build a race track," Dr. Hardwick admitted 27

years later. "But France invited a bunch of us down to the Firecracker 400 in Daytona to see what it was all about. We got down there and saw what an economic boost it was, and we said, 'This thing is on fire. This thing is red hot.' They had 65,000 or 70,000 people, and you couldn't get a motel for 50 miles around Daytona."

Leaders in the Talladega area caught "on fire" for the project, too. Hardwick, Hill, Travis McCaig, Kaiser Leonard, Bill Sullivan and other civic and political leaders began working to make possible the speedway that *The Birmingham News* said would "make the Birmingham-Talladega-Anniston area a United States auto racing center."

It did that—though it was built in a different configuration from the way France envisioned it that night in October. It was 2.66 miles long and faster than Daytona. It was a tri-oval, not a quad-oval. Ground wasn't broken until May of 1968, and the first race wasn't run until September of 1969. And it was named Alabama International Motor Speedway. Over the years most would refer to it simply as "Talladega," and eventually the name would be changed to Talladega Superspeedway.

AIMS grew out of a conversation between France and a racing fan. Bill Ward, an Anniston insurance man who had driven in a few minor events, was chatting with France when the stock car baron told him he was considering building a speedway in the Spartanburg, SC, area. Ward recalls the simple exchange went like this:

Ward: "Hell, build it in Alabama."

France: "Well, you find me 2,000 acres of land near an interstate, and I'll build it in Alabama."

Ward took him at his word and began scouting out the state—but he found a perfect location under his nose, a virtually abandoned airport that was once used by the U.S. government and later the city of Talladega. It was just off I-20.

"I went to the city of Talladega, and they didn't even know what I was talking about," Ward recalled. "I told the mayor to go to Daytona and see what I was talking about."

"The location was ideal," said France, who at the October meeting pointed out, "By 1972 the majority of the interstate

(left) A crane was used during construction of the speedway to produce its banked turns.
(below) An early aerial of the speedway shows the early stages of production, which began in 1969.

highways in the United States will be completed."

Later he explained: "Talladega is located within a 300-mile radius of a population of 20 million people, and it's stock car racing country. We wanted Talladega because we wanted to take the world's best racing to the people. That's why we built the world's greatest speedway where we did."

The old airport was built in 1942 to train Navy pilots, Hardwick said. The city of Talladega acquired it from the U.S. government for a dollar after it became surplus property "with the provisions we had to maintain a decent airport."

That was easier said than done. "We had three airstrips 5,200 feet long," Hardwick said. "They had poured the concrete in the winter of 1942, and it froze. It had a bad tendency to buck up. Weeds grew up in the thing.

"We finally got the FAA to let us abandon two of the strips and maintain just one. It was costing the city money to try to maintain it." The runway was unsafe, he said, and some planes had been damaged.

Finally, it was approved by all parties that 600 acres would be given to France's group in exchange for its building a new airstrip for Talladega. "We got an evaluation, and it was $800 an acre," Hardwick remembered. "We got the price of a brand new airstrip on the periphery, and the estimate was $480,000."

France leased some more land from the city and bought some from individuals. George Wallace, then governor of Alabama, cooperated enthusiastically on the project, and the state built a fine access road. Finally, a huge speedway rose on some 1,800 acres of land—the cost of the project in the neighborhood of $6 million.

"Dealing with France was easy," Hardwick said. "If it wasn't good for the city, it wasn't good for him. We had no problems whatsoever in dealing with him.

"Will Rogers said he never met a man he didn't like. The only man Bill France didn't like was the one who tried to cheat him the second time. He'd forgive the first time."

Bill France Jr., CEO of International Speedway Corp., said the speedway was constructed through money borrowed from a bank, "and we raised some equity with the UNOCAL Corp. We sold them part of International Speedway Corp. We later bought them out."

The course is banked 33 degrees in both the north and south ends, two degrees steeper than Daytona's, and it

was built a little longer than Daytona's. Why?

"We had enough land to do it all with," Bill France Jr. said. "It seemed like a good idea, and I think it has been."

The speedway was built by Moss-Thornton Co., an old Alabama firm. A ceremony was held on May 23, 1968, with Harley J. Earl, NASCAR national commissioner and retired vice president of General Motors, breaking ground for the speedway and Dr. Hardwick breaking ground for the new Talladega Municipal Airport adjacent to the track.

Today, Bill France Jr. remembers his late father as a man "with a lot of vision who got things done. He would tackle things though financing wasn't available at the time. He'd start without it and assume he'd find it as he went on. Most guys who try that end up in Chapter 11, but he never did. He was the king of the bootstrappers."

He understood finance, though. "He recognized that if you borrowed money you had to pay it back. He could figure the interest rate and recognize the debt service. He didn't finish high school, but he went far enough along to figure out the debt service was X and he could only pay Y. He didn't do dumb things."

Dr. Hardwick, who still practices medicine as a "pinch-hitter," was mayor of Talladega for 18 years, the last in 1973. He is pleased he was in office when the speedway was planned, built and opened. "I'm really proud of it," he said. "I've still got some pictures of me with the shovel in my hand at the groundbreaking."

The first Winston Cup race was scheduled for Sept. 14, 1969. It would be called the Talladega 500 in honor of the people of the area who had worked so diligently to get the speedway.

Ford Motor Co. even named a car the Talladega, which prompted Raymond Martin, mayor of the nearby town of Lincoln, to joke, "So what? Ford named a car for us long ago."

> *"Talladega is located within a 300-mile radius of a population of 20 million people, and it's stock car racing country."*

Richard Brickhouse, a young farmer from Rocky Point, NC, won the first Winston Cup event at Alabama International Motor Speedway. But the big story of the 1969 Talladega 500 was about who didn't race rather than who did.

Factory drivers and others announced the day before the 500 that they would boycott the race because tires were lasting just a few laps at the unprecedented high speeds made possible by the design of the new track.

Bill France Sr., president of International Speedway Corp., which operates the track, and president of NASCAR, announced that the race would be run without them.

A makeshift field of 13 Winston Cup cars and 23 Grand Touring automobiles contested the first Talladega 500. The lighter, slower GTs competed in the speedway's first event, the Bama 400, on Saturday, and France opened the next day's Talladega 500 to them. Ken Rush of High Point, NC, made history by winning the 400, the first race at the track.

A month before, the Professional Drivers Association had been formed, with Richard Petty as president. All the leading drivers except Bobby Isaac became members of the union.

Teams checked into the new speedway on Tuesday, Sept. 9. Charlie Glotzbach reached 199.987 miles an hour in practice, and he became the favorite to win the pole.

As crews fine-tuned their cars and speeds crept up, tire wear became more alarming. Glotzbach did win the pole, speeding 199.466 miles an hour in a radical, winged Dodge Daytona. LeeRoy Yarborough was second in a Ford Talladega at 199.350. Glotzbach was pleased to be on the pole, disappointed he hadn't gone faster. "I had expected to run 200 miles an hour," he said. "I really did."

Junior Johnson, owner of Yarborough's car, said, "We thought we might run 200, and I think we will before the week is out."

But as the week went on, the situation deteriorated. Serious wear had the tire companies trying various compounds, but it was apparent the Talladega 500 could not be safely contested at speeds near 200 miles an hour.

Glotzbach and Donnie Allison ran an impromptu tire test on Friday, driving several three-lap and five-lap stints and returning with tires in sad shape. Allison said he had never been more scared, and Glotzbach said the race should be postponed.

France called a press conference at 8 p.m. Friday. "We're going to run the race on Sunday," he said. "We've got a problem. Whether or not it's major, I don't know. As of right now, I don't think it's major."

Driver Bobby Allison was asked if tire wear was a major problem. "I think the biggest they ever saw," he answered. "They just can't stand the speed. The most we've gone is five laps on tires."

Cale Yarborough said his tires weren't lasting. "Sometimes they pull apart in three laps and sometimes they go six or eight laps."

On Saturday, Petty announced that PDA members would not compete in the next day's Talladega 500. France said the race would go on as scheduled.

Petty said the racing surface was rough and breaking up in spots and damaging cars and that tires would not hold up at the high speeds.

"The track was rushed up to get this date in, and the tire people didn't get the time that they needed to develop a tire for the track," he said. "It nobody's fault. There is nobody to blame. The track is just too new."

Said France: "We've got $125,000 posted for prize money. If one race car is there he will get first-place money. Anybody who wants to run can, and anybody who doesn't want to doesn't have to."

France contended the competitors should drive according to the conditions. If a pilot encountered bad weather he would fly his plane more slowly, he reasoned.

Don Schissler, a Grand Touring driver who started the 500, agreed. "Racing always has been according to a given set of conditions. You drive as fast as your equipment will permit. I could tear all the rubber off a car in 10 laps on a half-mile track if I chose to drive that way.

"So, if this track was too dangerous at 200 miles an hour, the thing for the big guys to do was not drive 200 miles an hour. It's that simple."

The boycotters found the idea of driving at slower speeds preposterous. "Who would you get to do that?" Bobby Allison asked.

A union statement said: "There isn't a PDA member alive who will deliberately run behind another driver

Brickhouse and his team savor the win in Talladega's first big race

when his car can run faster. Every serious race driver wants to win, right from the start. If full racing speeds could not be risked, the race could not be run in a proper way."

The Talladega boycott caused hard feelings and divisions, some of which healed and some of which didn't. There was even a difference of opinion in one family. Buck Baker drove in the race while his son Buddy pulled out.

"Things must have gotten a little plush for a lot of these guys, or they must want them a little better than they are," Buck said. "When I sign an entry blank, I'll race. I remember driving around holes in the tracks where you could bury a man."

France said he had a duty to spectators who had come for the 500 and to the drivers and car owners who wanted to compete, and so the race would go on. Fans could exchange their tickets for tickets to a future event at Talladega or Daytona and thus see two for the price of one.

Isaac was the only factory driver who competed and the pre-race favorite. Brickhouse, a sophomore on the circuit, resigned from the PDA before the 500, saying he hadn't dreamed it would be used for something "as erratic as boycotting a race." Glotzbach's pole-winning car was

withdrawn, but Brickhouse drove another Glotzbach Dodge, also owned by Nichels Engineering.

A crowd of 100,000 had been expected, but given the uncertainty, an estimated 62,000 showed up. They saw a competitive race driven at the speeds that were possible—a race without a wreck or a spinout.

Brickhouse, Isaac, Tiny Lund, Jim Vandiver and Ramo Stott fought a close battle, the lead changing hands 32 times. Brickhouse took it for good on the 178th lap of the 188-lap race and beat Vandiver by 250 yards to score what would be the only Winston Cup victory of his career. Stott finished third in the car Brickhouse originally was scheduled to drive, and Isaac, who had tire troubles, ran fourth, a lap down.

"I kept a lid on my speed most of the race," Brickhouse said. "But when I was behind in the late going I pumped my speed up to about 198 miles an hour to catch Vandiver."

His crew was concerned about tire wear, he said, and his chief "came all the way out on the grass to tell me to slow down. I ran hard enough to win, then I backed off."

It was obvious that big league stock car races would be run as scheduled, with or without the drivers who happened to be the stars of the time. There was never another strike, and the PDA eventually was disbanded.

1970

Pete Hamilton told some of his pals at Alabama International Motor Speedway to be sure and watch him on The Dating Game, a taped TV show that would be shown in a few days.

"I won a trip to the Kentucky Derby with a cute little girl," he said.

Her name?

"I forgot."

Hamilton never forgot the 1970 racing season, though. The 28-year-old college dropout from Dedham, MA, driving a Petty Enterprises Plymouth SuperBird, won the Daytona 500, the Alabama 500, and the Talladega 500 on NASCAR's biggest tracks.

Those would be three-fourths of the Winston Cup victories he would ever score. Chrysler cut back its racing program after the 1970 season, and Hamilton was one of the drivers who got the ax. Petty Enterprises would field a Plymouth for Richard Petty and a Dodge for Buddy Baker in 1971, Richard Petty announced. "We would like to keep Pete," he said, "but the word came from Chrysler."

Hamilton's career never sparkled after that magic season. He won one more Winston Cup race and eventually became a short-track car builder.

It was a disappointing turn of events for a fellow, who in 1970, was being compared to Fred Lorenzen, another blond bachelor from the north. In the early 1960s Lorenzen ventured south and became the first Winston Cup driver to earn $100,000 and win recognition as one of the sport's all-timers.

"Fred was a great race driver," Hamilton said after his victory in the Alabama 500. "But I'm trying to be my own race driver. If I were modeling myself after anybody, it would be Richard Petty."

Stock car racing entered a new era with the Alabama 500. It was the first time a crack field of factory-backed cars would compete at the world's fastest speedway. Most of the factory drivers and many independents pulled out before the inaugural race, the 1969 Talladega 500.

If you wanted to perplex the world's fastest stock car driver, Buddy Baker, you had only to ask him what to expect in the Alabama 500.

"I wish you had asked me any other question in the world," said Baker. "I don't think anybody knows.

"I don't think the tires will be any problem. But I feel the pace of the race will have a lot to do with the outcome of the race.

"Bobby Isaac and Dave Pearson and I ran over 200 miles an hour drafting Friday. If we are going to break loose and run 204 Sunday that could cause somebody problems.

"There's no question in my mind there will be some 200-mile-an-hour laps. I know that will happen. When you get three or four cars running in a line you can come on down the road."

On March 24, 1970, Baker ran tire tests for Goodyear in a Dodge Daytona. He exceeded 200 miles an hour three times, with a fastest lap of 200.447. Chrysler announced that he was the first driver to top 200 on a closed race course.

Baker said he expected a flat-out pace to win the Alabama 500, though many cars wouldn't be able to stand it. "Somebody's got to finish, running like that," he guessed.

Whatever happened, a national television audience would be peeping in. It was a time when a race on TV was a rare sight, but on Dec. 17, 1969, NASCAR and ABC-Sports signed a $1,365,000 contract that called for ABC to televise nine races in 1970, five of them live, but none flag-to-flag.

"This is certainly a major breakthrough for stock car racing," said Richard Howard, chairman of the NASCAR Television Committee. "The popularity of the sport has risen tremendously in the last few years, and now people all over the country will be able to enjoy NASCAR racing."

Roone Arledge, president of ABC Sports, said stock car racing segments were popular on the Wide World of Sports program, adding, "Viewer interest in the sport confirms our belief that the time is ripe for automobile racing's expansion on television."

The first of the live ABC telecasts was the Alabama 500, but the race was half over when the program began.

A crowd estimated at 36,000, many in on rain checks from the 1969 Talladega 500, saw Hamilton employ the Lorenzen style of playing it cool to win. He wasn't a leader until late, but he stayed in sight of the leaders and

Heavy traffic in the '70 Alabama 500.

when they dropped out he was there.

"You've got to have a car to race with at the end of the race," Hamilton explained. "If you run hard all day, it's hard to have any left at the end.

"We tried to run a certain speed. I was trying to pace myself, running the same RPMs all day. You've got to finish the race to win the race."

Hamilton got his opportunity on the 170th lap of the 188-lap event. Baker apparently would win, but then he pitted and took on four tires and lost a lap to Hamilton .

Then Pete stopped for right-side tires only. He came out of the pits leading Baker by a straightaway, but the faster Baker was gaining.

An oil cooler on Baker's car was struck by a piece of shredded tire, and Buddy's car burst into flames. He spun it down the straightaway, and Hamilton had his win.

"It's a very important part of the competition out here when you have to take the time to change four tires," Hamilton said. "We ran a different groove from the others and tried to save our tires. We ran higher in the turns.

"Richard and I tried to sit back there at the start and see what the tire situation would be. Tire wear picked up as the race went on.

"We didn't blister tires. We had no tire problems what-

soever, except I cut one. I had my hands full when the tire blew. I got sideways for about 200 yards. Evidently, I ran over something."

Hamilton was a lap behind at one point. He explained how he made it up: "I changed right side tires under green then caught a caution flag and came in and changed the left ones. I believe everybody else changed four at once."

Baker was treated for second-degree burns on his face and legs and was released from the track hospital.

"It was the scariest thing that has ever happened to me," he said. "Fire started rolling all over me. I could feel my legs burning, then the fire started rolling up my arms and licking me in the face. I was wondering what in the world I could do to get stopped before I cooked. Then I remembered that if you spin the car, the wind puts out the flames."

A Goodyear spokesman said the tires "seemed to perform pretty well" and that there certainly was nothing like the situation that led to the driver walkout of the year before. He said he was "disappointed a little" that there were some tire ailments.

NASCAR reduced speeds before the Talladega 500, and got the fastest 500-mile automobile race in history.

"Was it a record?" winner Pete Hamilton asked after he climbed from his car.

Yes, his 158.517-mile-an-hour tour broke the old NASCAR mark of 157.950 by LeeRoy Yarborough in the 1969 Daytona 500 and topped anything that had ever been done in the Indianapolis 500.

"Beautiful! That's what I wanted!" the 26-year-old Dedham, MA, driver exclaimed.

An asterisk would taint Hamilton's record, though. Richard Petty, his mentor and teammate, averaged 160.627 in the 1966 Daytona 500—but that race was called at 495 miles because of rain.

The Alabama 500 had been run in ideal April weather, and there had been no tire crisis, but the punishing heat of August in the Heart of Dixie was in the mix this time. NASCAR, drivers and Goodyear were concerned.

Less than a month before the race, Charlie Glotzbach and David Pearson had tested tires at Talladega. Two tires on Glotzbach's car wore out in just nine laps. A blowout sent Pearson's racer into the wall— and he was running only 192 miles an hour.

"Something's got to be done before we race down there again," Pearson said. "The tire people have done a lot for racing, and in time I'm sure they'll whip this problem, too. But until they do, something's got to be done."

If there wasn't a suitable tire for the race or if speeds weren't reduced, he would ask his car owner to withdraw his entry, Pearson said.

Something was done. On August 8 NASCAR announced that, beginning with the August 16 Yankee 400 at Michigan, cars would be equipped with a plate between the carburetor and intake manifold. The venturi openings would be reduced, and thus speed would be cut.

"Drivers and car owners have told us that they have been on the ragged edge at most of the races this year and have had trouble keeping their equipment together," said NASCAR's Lin Kuchler. "These changes should provide closer competition."

Bobby Isaac, who had set the all-time NASCAR qualifying record of 199.658 miles an hour for the Alabama

500, also won the pole for the Talladega 500—at a speed of 186.834 miles an hour.

But qualifying speeds frequently don't predict the average speed of a race, and a crowd estimated at 52,000 saw Peter Goodwill Hamilton drive his Petty Plymouth into victory lane in unprecedented time, giving him a sweep of both 1970 Talladega races.

It was an easy victory for Hamilton, Bearing no resemblance to his comeback win in the Alabama 500 four months before.

Hamilton shot to the front on the 20th lap and led 153 of the 188 laps. There was no laying back as he had done in April. He set a pace no one else could begin to match and won by nine seconds over Bobby Isaac. By the 100th lap the race had settled into a routine roundy-round with only Hamilton and Isaac in the lead lap.

Hamilton explained his charging in August versus his holding back in April: "The tire problems were more critical before for the speeds we were running, but we felt at these speeds we wouldn't have trouble."

Why was he so much faster than everyone else? "There were other cars that could run as fast as I could on fresh rubber, but as the tires wore down some of the other guys had to let up in the middle of the corner."

Hamilton liked the carburetor restrictor plates. "You could tell you were running slower," he said, "but I can't help but think it made a better race of it. As far as I was concerned, that was the best thing we could have done as far as competition, engine and tires."

Hamilton was so dominant that he couldn't resist the urge to make the car hum. When he was nearly a lap ahead at halfway, crew chief Maurice Petty tried to slow him down, but Hamilton ignored him.

The great Fred Lorenzen had retired in 1967, but it didn't take, and he returned to the circuit in Charlotte's World 600 in May. His engine blew early at Talladega, and he stood at Hamilton's pits and recalled his glory days.

"Pete should get out of that throttle and play it cool at about 183," Fearless Freddie said. "He would still be outrunning everybody. But I know how it is when your car is running good and you're young and eager.

"I can remember being in the position Pete is in—the

Pete Hamilton is all smiles after the 1970 Talladega sweep.

race in the palm of your hand if the car holds together. It's a great feeling. I'd like to experience that again.

"I don't know what happened to my racing luck. I used to finish about every race I entered. People used to say I won on strategy. I haven't lasted long enough to try any strategy since I started driving again."

Some other drivers weren't as fortunate with their tires as Hamilton was with his.

"I don't understand it," said a Goodyear representative during the race. "Pete is turning consistent laps of 187, and he had only a nick or two in his right front. Others are tearing up tires and only running around 180."

Leonard Wood, Cale Yarborough's crew chief, said, "We can't begin to race with Hamilton. We can't keep tires on our car anywhere near the speed he is running."

The unlikely leader in point standings when the Talladega 500 began was James Hylton, the definitive independent.

Hylton drove races to finish, not to win. Since the points system rewarded consistency more than winning, he found himself at the top.

Hylton recalled a race he did try to win at Nashville a few weeks before.

"It was the biggest mistake I've made this year, proba-

bly my biggest mistake since I've been racing," he said.

"I was running fourth and running good. The mechanics say they get tired of working on a car that isn't trying to win. So I broke a ball joint and wrecked. That's the bad part of being an independent. There are times when you can run, but when you try it that's what happens. I won't be trying that any more."

Hylton said the new carburetion rule was a blow to him. It supposedly would cut the expenses of racing by keeping more cars running—but Hylton wanted factory cars to drop out, not keep running.

"My chances for the championship are slim now, very slim," he said. "This will hurt me worse than anybody. It will slow them down enough so that running flat out is no problem for them but they have enough horsepower to outrun me."

Hylton finished 10th at Talladega, and Isaac's second-place run enabled him to take over the points lead. At the end of the season, Isaac was champ, Bobby Allison was second, and Hylton was third.

1971

The spring race at Talladega had a new name, and the big league stock car scene had a new sponsor for 1971.

NASCAR and R.J. Reynolds Tobacco Co. formed what the sport's foremost historian, Greg Fielden, called "the most fruitful and important relationship in the history of stock car racing."

The Winston brand of cigarettes would sponsor a 500-mile event at Talladega and post a point fund of $100,000.

NASCAR President Bill France called the $100,000 "one of the largest point funds in automobile racing history. It will be the largest point fund in NASCAR's 23-year history."

Reynolds also did extensive advertising in newspapers and on billboards to promote races.

The champion, Richard Petty, got $40,000 of the $100,000 the first year. Those were impressive figures in stock car racing those days, but by 1993, Winston was posting a $3 million point fund with a minimum of $1.25 million for the champion.

Also, there is the Winston all-star race, the Winston Million, and numerous other tie-ins between Winston and NASCAR. Obviously, it has been a sports marketing marriage made in heaven.

The first Winston 500 delighted Alabama fans. Hueytown brothers Donnie and Bobby Allison finished 1-2 in an event newspapers suggested might have been, at that time, the greatest auto race ever run. There were 46 lead changes among four drivers, with Donnie's car finishing 20 feet ahead of his brother's. The front bumper of Bobby's racer was a foot ahead of the one on Buddy Baker's car.

A crowd estimated at 63,500 saw the Allisons and Baker hook up in a draft at the start and fight within its confines virtually all afternoon. By halfway, Dave Marcis had joined the war, and he contested it well until his engine failed on the 182nd lap of the 188-lapper.

The race almost ended under caution.

Marcis' motor blew while he was running third. With only six laps to go, the Allisons and Baker raced to the yellow flag, aware that if the green never flew again the leader would be the winner. Donnie outran the other two, with Baker second.

The pace car crept around, hoping to allow the cleanup crew time to put the oil-dry on the track before the race ended.

The green flag and last-lap white flag waved simultaneously, signaling a drag race of more than a lap. Donnie held the lead, but Bobby inched ahead of Baker for second.

Donnie led the others into the final lap—but with the Talladega slingshot aimed at him, he wasn't comfortable with the position.

"I would have felt better if I had been second or third at that time," the driver of the Wood Brothers Mercury said.

But there were no stones in Bobby's and Buddy's slingshots, and Donnie completed 500 miles first by a relatively paper-thin margin.

When the green and white flags were displayed together, he simply floorboarded it and didn't even glance at his rearview mirror.

"The only thing I could do then was drag race them to the first turn," Donnie said. "I never looked back until I got back around to the finish line."

Donnie said he got "quite a jump" on Bobby and Baker when the green flag flew for the final lap. "I think Bobby being on the outside of Buddy made a big difference. It wasn't letting either one of them use enough race track."

The race almost ended under the caution with Donnie leading. "It didn't make any difference whether it did or not," he said. "I felt if I won, okay, and if not I had a reason for losing—somebody beat me."

The first Winston 500 was "a great race," Donnie said. "All day I figured the important thing was to be at the right place at the right time because anybody could lead to the finish line. This track is fabulous where drafting is concerned."

He added: "I guess this was the hardest race anybody ever ran for 500 miles."

Marcis' blown engine set up the first of two sprints to the finish line. "I looked up in the stands on the backstretch and saw the fans looking behind me, so I knew

Donnie Allison is interviewed following his win.

something had happened," Donnie said. "I knew I had to run for it."

Lap money was rarely worth the trouble in NASCAR races of that day, but the track paid $100 per lap, or $18,800, in the 1971 Winston 500.

Before the race, David Pearson's advice to his competitors—and himself—was to forget about the lap money.

"When they get to thinking about that $100 a lap they probably won't finish," Pearson said.

"It will probably make the boys who can lead push their cars harder. If they want to be around at the end of the race they had better forget the lap money."

As for himself: "I'm not worried about the lap money at all."

Donnie Allison, the pole sitter, was the man to beat, Pearson figured—but he also believed he could be beaten.

"He hasn't won yet, has he?" Pearson asked. "Donnie is a good driver, but you never know about racing. If you did, there wouldn't have been 60 or 70 cars out here this week."

Donnie Allison led 52 laps. "I ran the car about as hard as it would go all day," he said. "I'd drop back sometimes but, after all, they were paying $100. I told my crew before the race if I saw I would jeopardize my chances of winning by trying to lead I wouldn't do it.

"In order to have led this race all day you would have

had to have been a superman."

Donnie's car ran hot throughout the race. "I was afraid we would have to stop under the green and get water, but we didn't," he said.

It was the fourth time the Allison brothers had run 1-2—with Donnie winning every time.

"I got beat," Bobby Allison said. "It was the way the breaks went. Donnie drove a good race. It's like my dad said—second is better than what everybody else but one did."

Baker said: "It was one of those races where you have to grin and bear it—only I'm not grinning. I thought one of the four—the Allisons, myself, or Marcis—deserved to win it."

Marcis was driving for Bobby Isaac, who was hospitalized with kidney stones the day before. He fought a good fight before his engine blew and he spun out six laps from the end.

"I noticed the car bogging down as I came out of the fourth turn," Marcis said. "I thought maybe I was losing the draft, but the engine blew."

Marcis wasn't in contention early, but he caught up about midway through the race. "I had planned to try to get the lead at the start," he said, "but when I didn't I decided to drop back and get used to the car."

The 1971 season was the one that established Alabama International Motor Speedway as the most competitive track in auto racing.

There were 46 lead changes in the Winston 500, and everyone wondered what stock car racing could do for an encore. The answer was to produce a Talladega 500 with 54 lead changes—the most ever in any kind of auto race.

And again the result delighted the homestate fans. Bobby Allison won the Talladega 500, giving him and his Hueytown neighbor-brother Donnie Allison a sweep of the Talladega races for 1971.

They even qualified 1-2 for the Talladega 500, Donnie winning the pole, as he had for the 500. "They're the ones to beat," Buddy Baker said before the race. "But we knew that before we ever came down here. It looks like we might have to draft most of the day and hope for the breaks on pit stops."

The world's largest speedway was still new enough that its vacuum-cleaner draft was a curiosity and a widespread topic of conversation.

"I'll tell you one thing," Baker said before the race. "A cat who doesn't like to draft can go home now. That's all it will be."

Reflected Baker: "Drafting is an art in itself, because you pick up five miles an hour in just a second. Sometimes in the draft when you do something wrong you feel like somebody has hit you. But you look back and there's nobody within 50 feet of you.

"I think our car will free up some in traffic Sunday. I qualified at 178 for the last race here but ran 188 in traffic."

You almost had to draft to understand it, Baker indicated.

"When I try to explain drafting to someone who has never done it, it's like trying to explain roller skating to me if I've never done that. If you don't roller skate correctly you'll be on your seat, and if you don't draft correctly you'll be in trouble, too.

"In drafting, the other drivers can almost drive your car for you. They can make you go where they want you to."

Baker finished third in a duel with the Allisons in the 1971 Winston 500. He recalled losing the draft in the payoff sprint to the flag.

"I got caught out of the draft by the Allisons on the third turn of the last lap of the race. Bobby went high,

and Donnie went low, and they left me hitting the wall of air, and the funny thing was they didn't mean to do it that way.

"Bobby was like me. He didn't dream Donnie would go low. When Bobby got out from directly behind Donnie, it cost him a chance to win, too."

But nobody could beat Bobby Allison in the 1971 Talladega 500, though a tiny piece of debris tried.

A crowd estimated at 66,700 cursed an afternoon shower that drenched them, but for Allison, it was heaven sent. Without the rain, he might not have gotten his Holman-Moody Mercury into victory lane.

"I picked up something in my eye before the green flag ever fell at the start of the race," he said. "It was hurting pretty bad, and while the race was stopped for the rain I went to the doctor and had it taken out.

"I was getting pretty used to it, but I had decided if it got worse I would have Donnie relief drive for me. We had him in the pits standing by."

Bobby drove for an hour and 15 minutes with the object in his eye.

The forty-five minute delay for the track to dry provided him with another opportunity. He consulted with his brother, who had dropped out after just 44 laps, and got valuable advice.

"Donnie was definitely stronger than I was before he blew his engine," Bobby said. "During the rain he told me how he was running the track, and it helped me. But what he told me is a secret."

The outcome of the race wasn't settled until the drivers entered the third turn of the final lap.

They began the lap with the nose of Bobby's car two feet in front of the grille of Richard Petty's. Pete Hamilton's was on their bumpers.

Petty edged ahead of Allison in the second turn, but Allison regained the lead in the backstretch. In the third turn, with Allison barely in front, Petty and Hamilton collided. Hamilton spun into the infield. Petty's car fishtailed, and Allison sped to the tape to win by 2.2 seconds over Petty. Hamilton recovered to finish third since he was four laps ahead of Fred Lorenzen at the time.

"Anyone want to hear a loser?" Petty said with a grin

up," Allison replied. "Everybody saw the lapped car. The track is four lanes wide, and there wasn't but four of us. It seemed to me there was room for everybody, and I only moved up enough to clear the slow car.

"I feel real bad Pete was the victim. Pete has suffered from lack of equipment and everything else."

Petty said: "I've been driving a race car thirteen years, and the only person I ever had any run-in with is Bobby Allison. Anybody who would spin his own brother out in a 25-lap feature, you've got to watch out for them. Enough said."

Did Petty feel anything was done intentionally? "Enough said," he repeated, then added, "Everybody tries to win. Some just go about it in a different way."

Allison retaliated: "He's had trouble with Isaac, Pearson, Paschal, anybody who has ever run against him for any time. The trouble comes in neck-and-neck competition. Anybody who is too small to realize that is hurting his own self."

Petty told writers to "go check my car. That will explain what is going on. A lot of red paint is on my car."

Countered Allison: "I've got some blue on mine, so I imagine he has some red on his." Petty's Plymouth was blue, Allison's Mercury, red.

Could Petty have won the race if the incident hadn't occurred? "It would have been a damn right smart closer," he answered.

Second-place money made him the first stock car driver to earn $200,000 in a season. "I want to celebrate winning $200,000," Petty told the press box, breaking some of the tension. "Somebody give me an aspirin."

as he entered the press box after the race. But soon the mood had changed, and no one was grinning. Accusation matched accusation.

"Bobby was on the inside, and I was in the middle, and Pete was on the outside," Petty spoke of the late incident. "Pete was about a foot up on my car.

"When Bobby moved up, I moved up, and Pete was the one who wound up on the short end of the stick."

Petty said his car hit Hamilton's. "Once we touched, Bobby just went on."

"We were coming up on a lapped car, and I had to go

1972

What race fan wouldn't have liked to have been a fly on the wall of David Pearson's passenger car after the Winston 500?

Pearson and Bobby Isaac, who finished 1-2 in what one newspaper described as the "zaniest stock car race ever run," were fast friends. They played golf together on Monday before the race, then rode together from the Carolinas to Talladega. They returned home together, too.

"I told Isaac he'd have to hitchhike back if he beat me," Pearson said after the race. "But I think he'll probably be pretty quiet on the ride back now."

After he had had time to cool off, Isaac joked: "I'll probably have to listen to Pearson bragging how he won the race. But that's better than walking home."

And Isaac did, indeed, require some cool-off time. He played the lead role in the zaniest episode of the zany day.

But first some of the other goofy happenings:

A pickup truck overturned on one of the 33-degree-steep banks of the world's biggest speedway. Two men suffered minor injuries. A crew was putting down some oil-dry during a caution period when the vehicle tumbled off the cliff.

Country music star Marty Robbins finished 18th and was voted the top rookie of the race. He refused the award and the $250 that went with it, though, and asked NASCAR's technical inspector to check his carburetor—which NASCAR found to be illegal. The car ran much faster in the race than in qualifying, Robbins said. "I didn't start the race knowing the car was illegal," he declared. Robbins was disqualified, and the rookie award went to LeeRoy Yarborough.

Sixty-two laps (nearly a third of the 188) were run under caution, slowing the event to a creeping 134.400 miles an hour. Twice the Winston 500 was flagged to a stop because of rain.

The Isaac drama began after the second rain delay. All the leaders pitted when the yellow flag was displayed to signal the restart of the race. They hadn't been allowed to touch the cars during the red-flag rain stop.

A few laps later, on the 183rd circuit, NASCAR black-flagged Isaac because his gas cap was missing. Isaac, the leader, ignored the flag, refusing to come to the pits for consultation. Pearson was on his bumper.

In the fourth turn, on the next to last lap, Isaac attempted to lap Jimmy Crawford and their cars tangled, both hitting the wall. Pearson narrowly missed them and took the lead. A last-lap white flag and a yellow caution greeted Pearson, and he coasted to victory. Isaac continued and finished second.

NASCAR fined Isaac $1,500 for ignoring the black flag, but it allowed him to keep second place and its payoff of $15,895.

What if Isaac had won the race?

"That would be a different situation, and we probably would be meeting now," NASCAR official Lin Kuchler said.

Bill France Jr., facing his first crisis after succeeding his father as NASCAR's president, asked rhetorically: "How high is the sky? There'll be no answers to what-if questions."

Kuchler continued: "We had more than a half-dozen officials check out the gas cap. We took about five laps to be sure. When Isaac made his last pit stop, he started out of the pits and then stopped, and they ran out to put the cap on. The crew told us they had it back on."

Kuchler said the crew refused to signal Isaac to pit.

"There was no way I could race 500 miles at the speed and competition today and stop with four laps to go to get a gas cap," Isaac explained later.

"It seems like a pretty steep fine. I can't remember them fining anybody $1,500. I remember some fines of $100 to $500."

Pearson explained the key crash. The Spartanburg, SC, driver said Crawford "came up on a slow car. He moved up and squeezed Isaac into the wall. I saw it looked like it was going to happen, so I backed off and came pretty low. It was close. They were against the wall when I came by.

"Bobby was leading at the time, and that's what I wanted him to do. I was going to try to draft by him on the last lap. I had tried it before, coming off the fourth turn, and could beat him by about a foot, so I decided I'd better try it on the backstretch."

Pearson continued to race Isaac even though he saw Isaac's black flag. "I saw his gas cap off, and I saw them give him the flag two or three times, but I wasn't going to

Pearson displays the checkered flag after his first Talladega win.

degrees, then I'd pass him and let my car cool off. I felt I could draft by Isaac and take the lead when I wanted to, and I did.

"I figured it would be between Isaac and me. We were faster than everybody all week."

Pearson said he told a crewman on a stop that he wanted to be second or third on the last lap in order to slingshot around the leader and win the race.

"Anytime you were drafting anybody, you could run faster than they could because you could slingshot around," he said.

Isaac explained his wreck: "We were coming through turns three and four, and I was coming up on car No. 3. I got my nose by his quarter panel and saw him coming over. I tried to stop and get out of his way, but he came on over."

Did Isaac believe Pearson could have passed him on the last lap had there been no wreck? "It would have been awful hard. He was going to have to get an awful good shot at me to get by."

Unlike Pearson, Isaac said he would have tried to lead on the last lap rather than lay back and try for a slingshot.

take any chances," the driver of the Wood Brothers Mercury said.

If he had been in Isaac's place would he have heeded the black flag? "I don't know," Pearson said. "I thought about that. I guess he didn't know whether to come in and lose a few positions or just stay out there."

Pearson declared: "This was the best I've ever run on a superspeedway. Usually when you're running 190 miles an hour the car gets squirrely, but not today."

His strategy was to stay in a draft with Isaac. "We've been riding back and forth to the track together every day, but we never discussed that. We just did it.

"I'd run behind him until my car got up to about 200

The race was mostly Pearson and Isaac, but Buddy Baker hung in and finished third. Fred Lorenzen was the only other driver to complete 188 laps.

The 1972 Winston 500 was the first Winston Cup event for a young man named Darrell Waltrip. He got 38th place when his engine blew on lap 69.

It was the first Talladega race for Bill France, Jr. as president of NASCAR. His father, Big Bill France, retired from the post but remained president and chairman of the board of International Speedway Corp., which operates the track.

Mr. James Hylton didn't have the last laugh in the 1972 Talladega 500, but scoring one of the great upset victories in sports history did provide him with a side-splitting guffaw.

NASCAR instituted a new points system in 1972, one that rewarded laps completed. The independents loved it. They could buzz around the tracks at their reduced pace and pile up points while the big money teams, intent on winning, risked breakdowns.

When the tourists reached Talladega in May for the Winston 500, Hylton—Mr. Independent—was atop the points. If he could hold the lead through that race he would earn a bonus of $10,000. Bobby Allison was second, and Richard Petty was third.

The media didn't let Hylton—or the fans—forget that Petty had finished ahead of Hylton in nine of the 10 races and had won four times while the winless Hylton had simply accumulated lap points by completing all 10 races. NASCAR was embarrassed that Hylton was the leader, and grimaced at the possibility of having a champion who didn't visit a single victory lane.

"I didn't make the rules as to the points," Hylton replied to his critics. "I just run for them. If I had the money the other guys have, I could afford to run to win too. But I don't. I pay my own bills and have to make sure I earn enough money to go to the next race."

On the day before the Winston 500, Hylton, weary of the complaints, declared: "Maybe I'll blow and Petty will win and everybody will be happy."

Hylton's car, indeed, crashed early in the Winston 500. Petty took over the points lead and eventually won the championship, with Allison second and Hylton third.

"I should be the points champion because I'm leading in points," Petty said after that race. "James should be the lap champion. That's the difference. Actually, I admire him because he's figured out a way to beat the system. I really think NASCAR needs to look at the point deal."

But when the drivers returned to Talladega in the heat of August, it was James Harvey Hylton who was the surprise winner of the Talladega 500. It was one of just two Winston Cup events the Inman, SC, driver would ever win, and he started more than 600.

How big an upset was Hylton's victory? Well, on the

morning of the race a newspaper columnist quoted "odds" on drivers (David Pearson was the favorite at 3 to 1) and made Hylton 1,000 to 1.

But troubles struck the top dogs, and Hylton won. The second place finisher was an unlikely name, too. ARCA driver Ramo Stott's front bumper was alongside the back bumper of Hylton's Mercury at the stripe as a slingshot maneuver failed.

Bobby Allison was third, but the fourth, fifth, and sixth drivers were Red Farmer, Buddy Arrington, and Ben Arnold, little fish in Winston Cup's huge pond. Thirty-two of the 50 starters failed to finish.

Hylton said he came to Talladega to win, not stroke. "I got a lot of criticism on the points when all that got in the press," he commented. "It made it hard on my sponsor. But in Atlanta, when I broke a valve, that was it. I was out of the running for points then. I figured all I could do to make up the difference was win a race. We came down here to win this race."

Hylton decided the tire compound the drivers used in the Winston 500 in the spring was superior to the one Goodyear developed for the Talladega 500, and he raced on those tires. It was a wise decision, as the old tires were better. After the race started, some of the name teams tried to buy the Winston 500 tires from any independent outfit that might have them. Stott quickly switched from the new compound to the old.

A crowd estimated at 68,000 saw 30 official lead changes, but only Hylton and Stott led in the final 69 laps. Hylton was in front the last 39.

"I was just hoping I could put it together and not lose my cool on the last lap," Hylton said. "I thought of everything toward the end of the race. I'd go down the backstretch and hear something shake, and I'd look to see if the fenders were falling off.

"When they gave me the board that I was leading, I didn't believe it. I guess every dog has his day, but I didn't think I was ever going to have one."

Near the end, both Hylton and Stott felt Hylton would win the final sprint. "We had tried each other on the slingshot before, and I definitely had the fastest car," Hylton said. When he gained a draft from lapped cars on

Hylton pits for tires en route to victory in the '72 Talladega 500.

the last lap, he knew he would win.

"He had more horsepower," Stott said. "He was pulling me an extra three or four miles an hour. If I had been in front he would have had to put on his brakes to have kept from running over me. The third turn was my best place on the track. I could get by him there, but then he would go back around me."

Both cars got squirrely on the frontstretch on the last lap. "I got a little crossed up in the dogleg from looking in the mirror," Hylton said.

"It appeared he was coming closer and closer," Stott said. "I had to touch my brakes. He didn't need to go up as high as he did. The finish would have been a little closer. But I know James has worked hard a long time, and I'm glad to see him win a race."

Stott was pleased with second. "When I started the race I figured if I had a chance for sixth or seventh place I'd be lucky."

One by one the favorites suffered misfortune. A spectacular wreck on the 23rd lap eliminated pole-sitter Bobby Isaac. Petty dodged the accident but broke suspen-

sion parts when he hit the infield. Ignition problems sidelined Pearson, the favorite.

Buddy Baker's engine quit, and the car caught fire. Donnie Allison, who charged from 41st starting position to the lead in 35 laps, lost an engine. Motor failure stopped Pete Hamilton, and Bobby Allison nursed a sick engine to the end.

It was Hylton's second Winston Cup victory in 297 starts over eight years. He won a short track race at Richmond in 1970. It would be his last win.

"I'll never run for points again," Hylton said after winning at Talladega. "I've been concentrating on points, and that's where I was wrong. I'll concentrate 100 percent on winning.

"I'm going to run a lot harder than you've ever seen me run before. The $24,000 I won today is that first big break. You've got to have good equipment to run."

But reality set in, and soon Hylton was again running with the other independents.

"Not having bad luck is having good luck," David Pearson once reflected on his sport. Bad luck stayed away from his door in 1973, and he won an incredible 11 of 18 Winston Cup races.

There was bad luck in abundance at the Winston 500. It didn't hound Pearson alone. Twenty-one cars were involved in a crash on the backstretch on the 11th lap. They should have called it the Winston 28, for after just 28 miles Pearson virtually had it won.

The wreck sent his four principal challengers—Buddy Baker, Cale Yarborough, Bobby Allison and Richard Petty—to the showers, and after that all Pearson had to do was hold his Wood Brothers Mercury between the fences.

"It was one of our easier victories because all the guys went out early," the Spartanburg, SC, driver said.

Donnie Allison ran second. He pitted for tires in the opening laps, even before the big wreck, got a lap behind—and finished a lap behind.

Pearson was the race favorite anyway and with no serious challenger left in the field, he simply set an easy pace. "I ran about 188 the rest of the race, I think. I was doing 190, and they were pulling away from me before the wreck."

"The slower you run, the more apt you are to finish," his crew chief, Leonard Wood, said. "He just ran what the pace was."

It was the most calamitous crash in auto racing since the first lap of the 1966 Indianapolis 500 when half the field got scrambled. It sidelined 18 drivers and injured five. Wendell Scott was seriously hurt, and the wreck led to the finish of his career.

The accident was triggered when Ramo Stott's engine blew, oiling the racing surface. Cars began spinning off the pavement and kicking up a red dust storm that blocked the vision of drivers behind them.

The caution flag was displayed for 37 laps—for an hour and 25 minutes—after the wreck.

Pearson played it cool at the start of the race. He dropped back to let the other drivers determine the durability of the tires. When the carcasses of damaged cars

practically blocked the track, he brought his racer to a stop.

"When I got to turn No. 1, I saw the dust," Pearson recounted. "I slowed down to five miles an hour or may even have stopped when I got to No. 2. Cars were spinning all over the track.

"I saw a rear end, and I saw a front end on the track. And I saw the fender of one and the door of another one. I ran over something and busted a tire, but I knew I couldn't come in and pit then because I'd probably cut another tire when I went back around through that stuff. I knew I might as well wait until they cleaned it up. I ran I don't know how many laps with a flat tire."

Pearson didn't want to know if any of his opponents had lost their lives. "I thought some of them were hurt

pretty bad," he said, "so I didn't ask my pit crew. They're all my friends, and I thought it was better for me not to know. Then I'd be able to concentrate on the rest of the race."

Pearson was practically home free after the accident. "It's a relief knowing the fast cars are out," he said, "but I didn't want something like this to happen."

Sixty cars started the race, and Bobby Allison blamed the accident on the huge field and NASCAR's allowing racing to the flag in a caution situation. Allison said before the race that increasing the field by 10 cars added junk to the lineup.

"It was just an unfortunate racing accident," NASCAR President Bill France, Jr. replied. "I don't see that the 60 cars is related. As far as racing to the caution flag, I don't know how we'd police the he-passed-me-on-the-backstretch stuff.

"They weren't racing to the caution. They were trying to get stopped."

Yarborough had the distinction of being involved in the 1966 crash at Indianapolis and in the Talladega smashup. He called the Winston 500 wreck "by far the worst accident I have seen in 15 years of driving. It was the greatest miracle in auto racing that nobody was killed. There's enough junk here for a man to start a junkyard."

Said Baker: "We came off the second turn and saw

Pearson (21) and Buddy Baker (71) share front row in the '73 Winston 500.

cars, engines, tires, metal flying everywhere, and solid black smoke and dust was everywhere. I've never seen that many race cars wrecking in my life. Cale and I got up on the bank, and I promise you cars were wrecking for at least one minute."

"I had no place to go," Bobby Allison said. "Cars and tires flying everywhere. I just prayed I would come out of it."

Allison called it the worst wreck he had ever seen. "I was about stopped. I had hit someone enough that I could feel it. Then someone came and hit me. That started me down the track again, and I must have been going 100 miles an hour when I hit someone else.

"I was running good, too. I was just waiting for traffic to thin out some so I could really go."

Stott's engine blew, and his car hit the inside and outside walls. "I already had unbuckled my seat harness and had started to get out of the wrecked car," he said. "But then I saw it coming; cars spinning all over the place, ramming into each other, spewing tires, wheels, engines

and parts everywhere. So I decided to stay in the car."

James Hylton, who won the 1972 Talladega 500, wasn't so fortunate this time. "I was having another good day," he said. "I was back about 14th, but my car was running well. Then it happened. Before I knew it I was in a cloud of dust and couldn't see a thing. I got hit front and rear."

Gordon Johncock was another driver who was in the 1966 Indy smashup and the one at Talladega. "This is the worst I've ever seen," he said. "It was worse than Indianapolis. I remember that one. It started right on my car when a guy cut in and ran over my tire."

For some of the drivers, such as Walter Ballard, the wreck was a financial catastrophe. "My car looked like an accordion when they got through with it," Ballard said. "I'm out of business. But I've been out before. I'll get back somehow."

A crowd estimated at 80,000 saw the 1973 Winston 500 end, appropriately, under caution after Vic Parsons' engine blew two laps from the finish.

1973

Dick Brooks felt like crying after many a Winston Cup race. He did cry after the Talladega 500—but they were tears of joy that coursed down his cheeks.

Brooks was every bit as improbable a winner as James Hylton had been a year before. It was his first—and last—victory on the tour.

When Brooks got the five-laps-to-go sign from the flagman he thought, "If nothing happens to the car, I'm going to win."

When the flagman signaled one lap to go, Brooks said to himself, "Nothing can happen now."

When the checkered flag waved across the bow of his car, Brooks thought numbly, "That's great."

As his racer rolled toward the first turn, its 500-mile journey done, the full realization of what had happened struck Brooks.

"All of a sudden I started snubbing," he recalled. "I was crying, and I couldn't even see the turn. That's the reason I went around an extra lap when it was over. I didn't want to come to victory lane and have everybody see me like that.

"I've wanted it so long. My mother told me one time she remembered when I was just a little boy, I'd sit in the field with little toy cars and say 'udden-udden' until the veins popped out on my neck. Today I got to go 'udden-udden' all the way to the front."

Brooks brought a dream to Dry Valley. He didn't even know until Friday of race week he would be in the car, but he jumped into the racer, owned by two Georgia airline pilots and won. (Pete and Jimmy Crawford's hemi-powered Plymouth didn't have a driver,) and Brooks had arrived at the speedway and found the car he was supposed to drive wouldn't be ready, but...

Speedway management arranged a natural marriage, and Brooks became the wheelman of the black machine. Nobody raced Plymouths anymore, and the hemi had been pronounced dead. This particular car had never finished better than 16th. Brooks had no victories on the circuit and hadn't had a regular ride since 1971.

Obviously, there was no reason to expect great things from the entry. And after Brooks qualified 24th and someone asked him how he'd run, he replied, "As fast as it will go. But it won't last the race."

The car had a heating problem, so Brooks wasn't optimistic. He thought it could keep up with most of the others but that it would be in the garage before the checkered flag fell.

He was used to disappointments. He had come to the south from Porterville, CA, in 1969. "I had intentions of winning more races than anybody on the track," he remembered. "That was because I had never been around this kind of racing. I found out that it didn't work that way."

Disappointment followed disappointment, and Brooks finally decided to let it all ride with one toss of the dice. Unable to get a regular ride, he would build his own car. He lacked $7,000 when magic touched his life at Talladega.

"We haven't even figured out how to get it out of the garage," Brooks said with a laugh. "The garage has a little bitty door, and everybody is always asking when we're going to get it out. But it's going to be completed a lot sooner than I thought."

A crowd estimated at 70,000 saw 64 lead changes among 15 drivers. It was the most lead changes in the history of auto racing.

The spectators also saw Larry Smith, the 1972 Winston Cup Rookie of the Year, killed in a crash when his car hit the outside concrete wall in the first turn on the 14th lap.

Brooks' Plymouth ran with the leaders all day, but he lost a couple of laps on pit stops. He made them up during caution flags and beat Buddy Baker by 300 yards at the finish. David Pearson was a quarter-mile behind Baker.

A weird set of circumstances set up Brooks' victory. Baker and Pearson were in a tight duel with 12 laps to go when Baker's oil line broke. Smoke poured from his car, and the flagman waved the yellow flag.

Baker surprisingly continued in the race despite the billowing smoke. He stopped under yellow and took on oil. Brooks, who had been far behind, gained ground in the caution period and passed Pearson for the lead on the green restart.

Pearson's car had lost a valve, and it could only chug

Dick Brooks is exhausted after winning the '73 Talladega 500.

around the track as Brooks sailed to victory and Baker's smoking machine took second.

Pearson had been bidding to become stock car racing's second millionaire (Richard Petty was the first), but he came up $4,310 short. He did earn that distinction later in the season.

"Of the 188 laps, I ran 150 with it on the floor," Brooks said. "It was the first time I've ever been able to do that anywhere. Everything was perfect all day."

Smith was the first driver to die at Talladega, although the crash wasn't spectacular. In fact, it appeared that his car had hit the outside wall in a routine manner. Press, racing teams and public were stunned when the news spread that he had lost his life. Smith was pronounced dead on arrival at the track hospital, and a speedway spokesman said he had suffered "massive head injuries."

There was speculation that he had cut but had continued to drive on the inner liner, which finally blew, pitching his car into the wall.

Baker received the news of his death with stunned disbelief. "I just didn't know it was that bad," he said, shaking his head. "I thought he'd received a sprained ankle."

Raymond Williams ventured: "It's just the speeds. Some things happen to your car, and it can be bad. It was for Larry. There's nothing tricky about the first turn, though I was the first person to have an accident there in 1970."

It was at Talladega that Smith had first flashed signs of great promise. He finished 10th in the 1971 Talladega 500. He earned $24,215 on the circuit in 1972 and was named the Rookie of the Year (an honor that Brooks received in 1969).

"I could run sixth the rest of my life and nobody would notice me," Smith had said of his rookie award. "In the eyes of racing people, you're nobody until you become somebody. You can't become a somebody without winning. Now I've won something. Nothing big, but something.

"I've also learned to take the bitter with the sweet and how to work hard under a lot of pressure. If that means anything I'll be a winner. I like to think now that I'm somebody."

At the beginning of the Winston 500, a fox trotted across the track as if he owned the place. Maybe that was an omen, for David Pearson (called the Silver Fox because of the color of his hair and his effortless driving style) drove around the place as if he owned it.

The Winston 500 was one of seven superspeedway events Pearson would win in 1974, and though he beat Benny Parsons by just 20 feet, he clearly was in command all day.

"I could go to the front when I wanted to," said the driver of the Wood Brothers Mercury, who was the pre-race favorite.

The Winston 500, normally a 188-lap race, was contested for 170 laps over the 2.66-mile track (452.2 miles). Because of the international energy crisis, stock car racing cut back on the distance of some events in 1974. The Winston 500 was scored as a 188-lapper, though. It "started" on the 19th lap, by a trick of the pencil and of the imagination.

A crowd estimated at 75,000 to 80,000 saw Pearson breathe his little 351-cubic-inch engine much of the day. But twice in particular he dramatically demonstrated its strength, flexing its muscles like a boxer showing his biceps.

One occasion was when Gary Bettenhausen sped away to a big lead after a caution period. Pearson, without benefit of the draft, promptly ran him down.

Another was in the late laps when Pearson caught Parsons, who had beaten him out of the pits and taken a lead of more than three seconds. Pearson required just a couple of laps to pass him.

At the end, Parsons couldn't get close enough for a slingshot attempt, and Pearson won by 20 feet. "I felt the way he had run all day that I could outrun him," Pearson said.

NASCAR did away with carburetor restrictors in 1974. Smaller engines were given a carburetion advantage in the rules. "We are phasing out the high-performance big engines primarily because the Detroit manufacturers have done so," said Bill France Sr., NASCAR's founder. "We are sort of governed by the size they make and sell to the public."

There was a wide separation between the small and big

engines at Talladega. Pearson won the pole with a lap of 186.086 miles an hour. Buddy Baker's 426-cubic-inch hemi was the fastest big engine when he qualified at 179.060.

Yet there were some who believed the big engines might be more durable under the strain of racing at the world's fastest, biggest speedway. Richard Petty, who had used a 340 at Martinsville the week before, went to a 426 at Talladega.

Pearson's 351 served him well, however. "I was perfectly satisfied with the way my car was handling and running," he said. "I didn't know what the little engine would do, but that was all we worried about. We ran the same engine in the race that we ran in practice and qualifying.

"I kept close attention to the gauges all day long. We hadn't run the little engine on a track this big, and I didn't know whether it would last. This was a good test, and if it didn't come apart today it probably won't."

The little engine teased Pearson on restarts after caution periods, however. "All day long, after every caution, the others beat me on the takeoff," he said.

It was a typical Silver Fox race. Pearson dropped back at the beginning to survey the situation. "They were running a little faster than I wanted to run," the Spartanburg, SC, driver said. "I didn't want to rev the engine so much, so I just stayed back."

The race was halted by rain, but that didn't help his engine survive, Pearson said. "As a matter of fact, I've heard mechanics say that when you let an engine cool off and then start back the engine won't run as well. But we never had any trouble with it."

The crowd was delighted when the 40-year-old Pearson (who became a grandpa a few days before) pulled up beside the pace car, driven by Susan Goldwater, wife of Sen. Barry Goldwater. "I just wanted to get a little close to her and see how she liked it," Pearson said.

Pearson, Petty and Cale Yarborough won 28 of the 30 races in 1974, and Pearson said not having to race Petty in the Winston 500 gave him an unusual feeling. Petty finished third but never contended. "But it was good to know I could outrun him like I did today," Pearson said.

Two top challengers were the unlikely duo of Gary

The Wood Brothers team gets Pearson out of the pits quickly.

Bettenhausen, an Indianapolis driver, and George Follmer, known principally as a sports car man. Neither finished, though. "It would have been closer with them in there," Pearson said.

"If they had stayed in I might have dropped back to second or third place on the last lap and tried to draft by them."

Bettenhausen went out after Grant Adcox's car smashed into his pits, injuring three of Bettenhausen's crewmen, one severely. Don Miller was rushed to an Anniston hospital, and his right leg was amputated.

Bettenhausen's racer was in the pits when Adcox pulled in and lost control on the wet pavement after a rain delay. Adcox was treated for shock.

The event was stopped twice by rain, and the checkered flag didn't wave until five hours and 35 minutes after the start. It was 6:35, and twilight was settling over the rural Alabama countryside.

There were 53 lead changes among 13 drivers, Pearson leading 12 times for 58 laps. Unknown Dan Daughtry, who had surprised the fans by qualifying fourth, did it again by bolting to an early lead, but his car soon failed.

The energy crisis, forced by the OPEC nations, led to unprecedented gasoline prices, closed service stations on weekends, long lines at gas pumps and frayed nerves.

Auto racing ranked seventh among leisure-time activities in causing fuel to be used, but it was a highly visible consumer. A football team would gulp considerably more fuel in flying from coast to coast than would be burned in a 500-mile race, but racing officials knew angry citizens who couldn't buy gasoline for their passenger cars would scream that auto racing, not football, should be closed down.

So the National Motorsports Committee was formed to assemble figures on petroleum consumption and make the statistics available to the Federal Energy Office—and to the public.

The Federal Energy Office praised auto racing for compiling the revealing figures and asked all major sports groups to reduce fuel usage by 20 to 25 percent.

The Winston Cup series condensed practice and qualifying, reduced some starting fields and cut the length of the first 15 events.

And that's how the 1974 Winston 500 became the Winston 452.2.

King Richard Petty finally added AIMS to his kingdom by winning the Talladega 500, but reporters divided their time between covering the competition and scratching for information about an incredible pre-race incident.

More than a dozen race cars, perhaps as many as 20, were sabotaged in the speedway garage. Crews arrived the morning of the race to find fan belts and tires cut, toe-ins changed, oil lines twisted and foreign materials such as sand, water, dirt and soft drinks introduced into fuel cells.

The cars of the first six qualifiers—David Pearson, Petty, Donnie Allison, Buddy Baker, Neil Castles and Bobby Allison—were among those which had suffered tampering.

"One thing I'm sure of," said Talladega County Sheriff Gene Mitchell. "It was somebody who knew something about race cars."

The open garage was in a space of about three acres that was enclosed by a high wire fence. Mitchell said two auxiliary deputies were inside the zone all night and that at times the number reached four. They walked the area, he said.

Mitchell told reporters that someone may have remained inside the section, possibly hiding in a van, after it closed.

Roger Penske, owner of Bobby Allison's car, may have been first to notice something was awry. He spotted what appeared to be chicken feed in the area of the fuel cell. Other crews were alerted, and they began checking their cars and finding vandalism.

Allison said his crew required about an hour and a half to get his car back in running order. "The last time we ran here," he added, "we had some trouble, but we didn't find out about it until after the race. We found about three handfuls of trash in our tank. We were using a big Indianapolis-type filter, though, so none of the stuff got into the carburetor."

All the cars started the race, but some drivers and crews blamed the saboteur or saboteurs for problems encountered afterward.

Joe Frasson was furious after he fell out. "We could have won this race," he spat. "The car was really running. We'd qualified well. I said before the race that if everything held together we could win it.

"Someone took the bolts out of our oil pan. We found

that in time. But somebody messed with the oil line and twisted a fitting that made us lose oil. It was pumping out all under the car."

Neil Castles came in when he noted an oil problem. "It's got to be a very sick man," Castles observed. "He's not dealing just with cars, he's dealing with the lives of 50 people."

Castles hated to think of what could have happened. "If my oil had hit one of the tires there would have been a spin, and in that early jam there's no telling what would have happened."

Racing people shuddered at the very real possibility that the vandal or vandals was one of their own.

"I can't believe that it's any of the drivers, the owners or the crewmen," said Dennis McClellan, a member of driver Frank Warren's crew. "We're all so close. We're together every week. We borrow from each other. We stay at the same motels. We eat together. "Somebody's real sick."

McClellan said his car wasn't tampered with the night before. "I think they must have heard us squawking. The morning of qualifying, we rechecked our front end and noticed that someone had changed our toe-in. This wasn't anything new for us, either. We'd found five loose lug nuts at Daytona and two at Atlanta. We talked pretty strongly about it to the inspectors here."

No one was ever charged with sabotaging the cars at Talladega. The speedway beefed up its security in the garage area after the incident.

A rainy-day crowd estimated at 65,000 saw Petty edge Pearson by half the length of a front fender to win the race.

The finish was set up by a late caution flag. Petty was 10 seconds ahead of Pearson when Jackie Rogers' engine blew on the 178th lap of the 188-lap event, allowing Pearson to catch up.

Full-bore racing resumed on the 183rd lap, and Pearson took the lead. He maintained it until the last lap.

As they zoomed down the frontstretch for the final time, Petty feinted to the outside, then stuck his car under Pearson's. The racers scraped sides, and as they completed the journey.

Petty groaned when the yellow was displayed near the

Richard Petty in victory lane after his first Talladega win.

end, but the driver of the Petty Enterprises Dodge figured all's well that ends well. "The caution flag came out, and I said, 'Oh, oh, this is going to mess me up," he related. "And it did, I guess, until the last two feet of the race."

Pearson hadn't wanted to be in front, he said, but with Bobby Allison on his tail he was forced to pass Petty on the 183rd lap.

The draft was so strong, the slingshot so effective, that he knew he would lose when he entered the final circuit in the lead.

Pearson had added to his reputation as a fox in the Firecracker 400 at Daytona a few weeks before. He was leading on the last lap, but he slowed as if he had car trouble, and Petty passed him. Pearson then sped up, caught Petty, and slingshot around him to win. Petty called it a dangerous move.

"I wasn't thinking about revenge at all," was the Randleman, NC, driver's answer to an obvious question after he beat Pearson at Talladega. "I still ran second at Daytona, and winning here doesn't change that.

"I've outrun David a bunch of times, and he's outrun me a bunch of times, and if we keep racing that will hap-

pen a bunch more times."

Petty added, "If it happens to be your day, you'll win; if not, you won't."

He appeared to make it his day at Talladega, though. "I tried two or three moves on the last lap," Petty said. "He was trying to watch me to keep me from coming by. I moved up like I was going to pass on the outside, then he moved up, and I went under him. Our cars touched, and he had to get off of it."

Did Petty consider it a case of Pearson's coming down on him or his moving up on Pearson? "It was a little bit of both, I guess. I wanted to take up as much room as I could, and I suppose he did, too."

Buddy Baker—who would enjoy great helpings of success and misfortune at Talladega over the years—was leading near the finish when the rear end of his racer went sour. "David was faster than me, but Buddy was faster than both of us," Petty said. "Under the same circumstances, I couldn't have beaten Buddy."

1975

Stock car racing had undergone quite a spit shine in recent years. Benny Parsons wrote sensitive poetry and was president of his PTA. Buddy Baker was an Easter Seals chairman. Richard Petty spoke to church groups. Bobby Allison was at home standing before the Kiwanis Club.

But the hard-down-knocks nature of the game still surfaced, as it did on the frontstretch of the last lap of the Winston 500.

A crowd estimated at 75,000 saw Buddy Baker hold off David Pearson to win by two feet.

Pearson attempted to slingshot Baker on the frontstretch of the final circuit. He went to the outside, but Baker moved over, blocking the way. Pearson whizzed to the inside and pulled alongside Baker, but he came up a couple of feet short.

"I had been running high through there," Baker said without passion 30 minutes after the finish. "When I moved over I didn't know where Pearson was."

Said Pearson: "I could have taken him by slingshotting past on the high side, but he shut me off by forcing me too high. I didn't know whether he saw me or not, but I had to back out of it or run into the wall."

Would Pearson have done the same if he had been leading? "Yeah, I guess I would have," he answered.

Baker, who hadn't been in a victory lane since mid-1973, drove like ... well, like a fellow who hadn't been in a victory lane since mid-1973.

"I said, 'Lord, don't let him catch up before I get to that checkered flag'." Baker offered with plenty of passion. "I could see it waving, and I didn't want it to fall on his head. He's won enough for awhile."

The fans in the grandstand could see the tension in the body of the man in the Bud Moore Ford as he drove the last couple of circuits. "With $25,000 a couple of laps away, you'd be tense, too," Baker said. "I got right up over the steering wheel. I didn't want to make any mistakes."

A car that handled superbly enabled Baker to ride low on the track, pick up the draft from several lapped cars and stay ahead of Pearson for the last few laps.

"It was the best handling car I've ever driven on a superspeedway," Baker said. "That's the reason I could

move to the bottom of the track and get their draft."

Baker led the last 18 laps of the race, disdaining lead swapping with Pearson.

"I was worried about us running out of fuel," Bud Moore, Baker's chief mechanic, said. "I wanted him to draft Pearson for a few laps to save fuel. But he said he couldn't because the car would overheat—so I told him to get his best hold."

"The water temperature shot up to critical when I drafted Pearson," Baker said. "I just couldn't run second. So I called Bud and told him I was going to shoot the works."

The big Charlotte driver's day almost ended in the opening minutes of the race. Donnie Allison's engine blew on the 12th lap, and Baker's car hit the oil. "I ran sideways 150 yards before I was able to save it," Baker said.

The victory may have been even sweeter for Moore than for Baker. It was his first trip to a victory lane since 1966 when Darel Dieringer won the Southern 500 in his car. And it broke another drought. It was the first win for Ford on the Winston Cup circuit since 1971.

Moore enjoyed the rare experience of putting pressure on the Wood Brothers, Pearson's crew, which was the most famous in automobile racing.

Some 25 laps from the end, Moore's men changed two right-side tires and gassed Baker's car in what was then an unbelievable 12.4 seconds. When Pearson pitted on the next lap, the Woods didn't change tires. The fresher tires may have given Baker the edge he needed.

"The reason they didn't change tires was because we didn't give them a chance," Moore said. "After our stop they knew they had to gamble." He believed his men handled the Wood Brothers "real well."

There were 52 lead changes among a dozen drivers in one of the most competitive auto races ever contested. The speedway was becoming well established as the most competitive in racing.

Baker, Pearson, Richard Petty, Darrell Waltrip and Dick Brooks stayed locked in a five-car draft much of the day, ping-ponging the lead among them.

A wheel bearing problem put Petty out of the running.

Buddy Baker is a happy man after his first Talladega victory.

Then, some 25 laps from the finish, the four survivors pitted under green. Waltrip and Brooks got separated from Baker and Pearson, and it became a two-car race.

Pearson would have loved to have had the last lap to play over. "I should never have gone to the outside," he said. "There was not enough room. I had the apron on the inside that I could have worked with."

It was a neat win for Elzie Wylie Baker Jr. and Bud Moore, for Elzie Wylie Baker Sr.—Buck Baker—had given Moore some of his finest moments when he drove Moore's cars to Winston Cup championships in 1956 and 1957.

The Winston 500 was scarred by a freak accident in the pits that killed Richard Petty's brother-in-law, 21-year-old Randy Owens.

Petty's wheel bearing went out, and a fire developed in the wheel. Petty pitted on the 140th lap, and Maurice Petty, Richard's brother and chief mechanic, yelled for someone to douse the flames.

Owens, the brother of Richard Petty's wife Lynda, responded with a pressurized water tank. The tank exploded, flying 30 feet into the air and sending Owens 20 feet into the air, eyewitnesses estimated.

Owens, the father of two small boys, was pronounced dead of a fractured skull. Gary Rodgers, a member of Benny Parsons' crew, suffered a head laceration when he was hit by a jagged piece of the tank.

"I had just gotten out of the car," a shaken Petty said later, "and was stepping across the pit wall. Randy reached over to turn the pressure on, and the thing blew up."

Petty, who retired his car for the day, was baffled by the wheel bearing problem that had led to the incident and stunned by the young man's death.

"You could go up and down the garage area and ask mechanics, and all of them would say a wheel bearing problem was impossible in that car," he remarked.

"This is really getting close to home. He was just a kid, and he's got those two little bitty boys. The bad part of it is that somewhere down the line it could have been prevented."

The body of Owens, who had joined the crew four years before, was flown back to Randleman, NC, with Petty and Bill Frazier, the chaplain of stock car racing, accompanying.

1975

Fans who don't remember that Buddy Baker won the 1975 summer race at Talladega remember that Tiny Lund lost his life in that event.

Baker's Ford and Richard Petty's Dodge finished side by side, the Gentle Giant winning by about three feet.

But the stock car racing world was stunned by the death of another big man. Dwayne Lund, 6-5, 265, was killed when, on the sixth lap, his car was T-boned on the driver's side by one driven by Terry Link.

Lund wasn't lavishly successful as a racer. In fact, the label of Sportsman driver fit him just as well as that of Winston Cup driver. But his size—Japanese fans considered him a lovable curiosity when he raced in their country—and his charging style endeared him to the public.

And he gained fame as the hero in a drama that was so unlikely that even Hollywood wouldn't have touched it. In this instance, the word "hero" is used literally.

The Daytona Continental was a sports car race that traditionally opened Speed Weeks, and Marvin Panch was practicing for the 1963 event in a Maserati. Lund was watching as the car flipped and burst into flames.

Lund and four other men ran to the scene of the accident, lifted the burning machine and pulled Panch to safety. It was an act of bravery for which they received the Carnegie Medal for Heroism.

Panch was the driver of the Wood Brothers Ford, one of the top rides in Winston Cup racing. From his hospital bed, where he was being treated for burns, he suggested that owner Glen Wood let Lund drive the car in the Daytona 500.

Lund won the 500, and the public was captivated by the tale of the hero who got his just reward.

It was his first Winston Cup victory—but it was not to be the first step on the ladder to big league stardom. Lund won just two more Winston Cup events, both minor races. It was in sportsman and Grand American competition that he excelled.

In fact, he drove in three sportsman races between August 10, the day the rained-out Talladega 500 originally was scheduled, and August 17, the day it was contested.

He won at Summerville, SC, on Wednesday, blew an

engine at Savannah on Friday and finished fifth at Hickory, NC, on Saturday night. After the Hickory race, he flew back to Talladega with Bobby Allison in Bobby's Aerostar.

Life was pretty good for him, he told Allison. His sportsman racing was going well, and so was his fishing camp on Lake Moultrie in South Carolina. But he felt he was making a mistake to return to Talladega because his car wasn't capable of racing among the frontrunners. But he had promised the owners he would drive it, and so he would.

Lund had once told a journalist he was uncomfortable on superspeedways in equipment that wasn't top notch. So many cars didn't handle well, he said. If you got in one that did, well, that was one thing, but to "have to brave one lap after another like I've had to do so long, it's uncomfortable."

The fatal crash began when the 45-year-old Lund's car tagged the rear of J.D. McDuffie's. It spun, and Link's racer pounded it.

"Tiny tried to drop in behind me," McDuffie explained, "but he clipped my rear and got me sideways. I saw Walter Ballard spin to the inside, and Link had no place to go. It all happened so fast, we were traveling so fast, there was nothing anybody could do."

Baker and Lund were fishing buddies. Baker had not been told of Tiny's death, and when he learned of it at the post-race press conference he left the area and wept, later returning for the interview. "This is terrible," the Charlotte driver said. "It takes all the joy out of winning this race."

The dramatic finish was set up when Joe Mihalic's engine blew on lap 178 of the 188-lap race. That bunched the racers of Baker, Petty and Donnie Allison for a wild chase to the finish.

But an estimated 70,000 saw Allison's chances die when his right front tire started going down under caution. He limped around after the green flag dropped, turned into the pits for a tire change and saved third place.

The oil pressure on Baker's Bud Moore Ford was dropping, but he had the fastest car. Petty tried to go under him on the frontstretch of the last lap, but he didn't have the power to make the slingshot.

"I never saw Richard until about 30 yards from the fin-

Baker (15) and Dave Marcis (71) lead the pack in the '75 Talladega 500.

ish line," Baker said. "I thought he would come low, and he did. I was as low on the race track as you can go. He came up to my door handle, but he couldn't outrun me.

"I remember two years ago at Daytona when he beat David Pearson by going low off the last turn. He wouldn't have won that race if he hadn't gone on the grass. I didn't figure he would go on the grass at Talladega."

Baker was asked what strategy he had planned for the last stages, whether he wanted to lead or follow.

"To be frank, I didn't know what to do," he answered. "He passed me at Daytona with nine laps to go and rode off into the sunset. When he didn't come this time I figured I was a little faster. With two or three laps to go, I moved all over the track and checked my mirror to see where Richard would go. It was kinda like shadow boxing. I wanted to see where his strength was."

So, believing he had the faster car, Baker decided to lead rather than drop back and attempt the slingshot. "I'll tell you one thing," he said through a grin, "when you take the white flag and you're in front, you'd better comeback around in front."

The sinking oil pressure worried Baker. "Anytime you

have an oil problem you can burn a valve in the engine," he said. "Pressure should hold at about 75 pounds all around the track, but it dropped to 10 or 15 pounds. I discovered the pressure fluctuated more if I backed off in the corners, so I finally decided to let it go. If I was gonna go, I was gonna go in style."

The only place he went was to Talladega's victory lane—for the second time in 1975.

"He was far too fast for me," Petty said. "He put a lower move on me the final lap, but it wouldn't have made any difference. I tried all I could but just couldn't get there. On the restart, he just put the hammer down.

"I guess I was just trying to make it look good for the fans at the end with the dive down low. It wasn't that close."

Donnie Allison said he told himself his tire wasn't flat, but he knew it was. "I don't think I could have beaten Baker," he said, "but I might could have beaten Petty."

The quote has been attributed to several of his opponents. Maybe it was Tiny Lund who said, "Give Buddy Baker an anvil in the morning, and he'll break it before noon."

Baker did inflict terminal illness on some cars, but the fans knew one thing about him, and they loved it: Buddy Baker always was trying to win.

"I drive flat out and half turned over," Baker once said, "but I don't apologize. You wouldn't ask Joe Frazier to fight like Ali, would you? There have been some low spots—racing has broken my shoulder, my leg, my spirit—but I've been able to do things my way, and I'm proud of that. I've always managed to stay about one foot off the valley floor."

Humpy Wheeler, president of Charlotte Motor Speedway, once characterized Buddy this way: "When the green flag drops, Baker's eyes turn red. He's intense and headstrong, which are perfectly normal feelings for somebody who works in a hostile environment at speeds up to 200 miles an hour.

"He's an absolute master of the unexpected. There's not one other driver out there who isn't scared when Buddy's behind him. Nobody knows what he's going to do, probably including Baker. He is the only top driver down here who can sell tickets without winning races."

The man with the lead right foot loved Talladega, and for the most part, the track loved him, though they did have a few spats. He won four of the first 22 Winston Cup events at the world's fastest speedway. And in 1975 and 1976 he enjoyed an incredible streak of three straight victories. He took the Winston 500 and Talladega 500 of 1975 and the Winston 500 of 1976.

The chances of nailing three straight anywhere are terrible, but at Talladega, the most unpredictable track in the world? Baker knew the score.

"The odds are just so phenomenal against winning three in a row," he said after the 1976 Winston 500. "I think it was the first 500-mile race I was ever in that I didn't feel like I'd win it when it started. Everybody was telling me I was not going to win—and you start to believe it."

But Baker not only won, he drove the fastest 500 miles anyone ever had. His speed of 169.887 miles an hour surpassed Mark Donohue's 1972 Indianapolis 500 record of 162.962.

Baker finished 35 seconds ahead of Cale Yarborough. It wasn't a typical Talladega afternoon of lead swapping. The big Charlotte driver's Bud Moore-owned Ford led 135 of the 188 laps. He and Yarborough were the only two who finished in the lead lap. Bobby Allison was third, a lap behind, and Richard Petty was fourth, two laps down.

A crowd estimated at 80,000 saw the caution flag wave just three times for 14 laps—a situation that created the record speed and that was most disquieting to Petty.

Petty carried a heavy millstone all afternoon. Darrell Bryant wrecked on the 15th lap, and that produced a caution period. Petty made a routine stop, but his car stalled on pit road. His crew frantically pushed the racer, but before it restarted Petty had lost a lap.

His efforts to catch up provided most of the afternoon's drama. Petty and his fans hoped for gap-closing help from the caution flag, but none flew for the final 130 laps.

Petty made up ground under a yellow flag that waved on the 53rd lap, and 95 laps from the finish he unlapped himself. That accomplishment furnished the day's most exciting racing. Petty and Baker ran side by side for several laps, the sides of their cars banging together.

Finally, Baker waved Petty on and dropped back. "With a lap lead there was no point in racing that hard," Baker said. "I called Bud on the radio and told him I was going to sit back, and he said that suited him.

"If it had been anybody but Richard I would have been worried. We touched four or five times. We were studying each other in case there would be a last-lap run."

Petty led the race a couple of times but only when Baker made pit stops. And Petty had to match him stop for stop.

Baker was able to maintain an actual advantage of about half a lap, and finally, Petty's charge took its toll. His engine began missing, and he made a late pit stop that cost him another lap.

Baker, of course, wished as hard for the green flag to stay out as Petty did for the yellow to be displayed.

"The last 20 laps were the longest of my life," he said.

The winner qualified 12th. "Two nights ago, Bud Moore and all the crew just took the engine back to Spartanburg and built it back up," Baker said.

Buddy did experience one close call. "Somebody blew a motor going into the No. 2 turn," he said, "and it was kind of a question mark with me. My car got sideways."

Baker was pleased that just 40 cars started the Winston 500. In the past, fields of 50 and 60 cars had raced at Talladega. "When you have the 40 best you improve the field," he said. "Just look at the few caution flags. If you'd had 60 cars, there would have been twice as many caution flags."

Yarborough drafted all day en route to his runner-up finish. "Man, I've got a sore thumb from hitchhiking," he said. "I knew that was my only chance, and I could run in a draft with any of them even if it did seem to me they were 10 or 15 miles an hour faster than my car without the draft. That may be stretching it a bit, but I flat couldn't keep up without the draft."

Buddy Baker learned racing at the knee of his father, the great Buck Baker. Buck once said he preferred racing to his earlier job of driving a bus in Charlotte because in racing, the traffic moved in just one direction.

At 57, Buck was in the Talladega field, attempting a comeback. His engine failed, and his son was able to check on him via a contraption that was relatively new to racing.

"When he blew I called Bud on the radio and asked him if everything was okay," Buddy explained. "These radios are great. They ease a lot of people's minds."

"I kept saying, 'No, don't let a caution flag come out.'"

Baker looked like a man who had driven 500 miles but not like one who had won a 500-mile race.

"I want to apologize for one thing," he told the writers. "If I don't seem happy, it's not true. I'm just so tired, and I usually don't get tired in a superspeedway race.

"But I was hoping there wouldn't be a caution, and you can always make a mistake at Talladega, and that was just a double load on me.

"I really go down when I do win because I try so hard. In victory circle they said, 'Well, act like you've won something'."

It was a happy ending to a story that began ominously.

When the 1976 edition ended, there had been eight different winners in eight Talladega 500s, and for half of them—Richard Brickhouse, James Hylton, Dick Brooks and Dave Marcis—the victory had been their first on a superspeedway. Talk about an unpredictable race track.

Buddy Baker was bidding for his fourth straight Talladega decision in the summer of '76, but it wasn't to be. He was riding on leader Marcis' rear bumper on the 184th lap of the 188-lap event when his fuel needle dropped to China, and he was forced into the pits for a quick squirt of gas.

Freed of his final challenger, Marcis had only to hold the K&K Insurance Dodge between the ditches to win, and he did.

"By golly, we finally got one!" Marcis shouted into his radio as his car crossed the finish line.

"Be careful and don't wreck it going to the winner's circle," chief mechanic Harry Hyde cautioned from the other end.

Hyde couldn't be blamed for holding his breath. The big track had chewed him up and spat him out over the years.

"It's hard for me to be excited," Hyde said calmly, "because I've paid one hell of a price for this win. We've lost at least five automobiles here, and we've dropped out with three laps or five laps or one lap to go."

Perhaps Hyde's most exasperating moment at Talladega occurred a few years before when his driver—Baker—demolished his car on the very first practice lap of the week.

Hyde's Dodges had started on the pole in eight of the 15 Winston Cup events at the monster track, but until this one the finishing position had never matched the No. 1 starting spot.

But in this race Hyde not only had the satisfaction of seeing his car win, he knew he had masterminded the victory. The cliché that races are won in the pits is rarely true, but this time it was.

"Before the race, Harry said we'd stay a couple of laps behind everybody on pit stops if we could," Marcis explained. The strategy was to build a fuel cushion. "You can see how brilliantly it worked."

Hyde admitted that in doing so he cut it dangerously

close. In fact, on one occasion, when Marcis suggested he stay out one more lap before refueling, Hyde shouted, "You're out of gas now!"

Goodyear records showed Baker pitting on the 38th lap under green, the 57th under yellow, the 95th under green, the 110th under yellow, the 150th under green, and the 184th under green.

Marcis, indeed, stretched it out. He pitted on the 42nd under green, the 60th under yellow, the 99th under green, the 113th under yellow, and the 155th under green.

"We ran out of gas," Baker said. "The fuel pressure dropped, and we decided to come on in and pit and take second rather than 10th. I was the first one to pit every time, and you can't do that."

Baker said his crew "miscalculated" in making early stops. "I take the blame when it's my fault, and when it's theirs I give it back to them."

Baker believed he would have passed Marcis and won the race if his tank hadn't gone dry.

"We knew it would be close as to whether I could make it to the finish without gas," said Baker. "That's why I was trying to draft Marcis near the end. I tested him to the right and tested him to the left. I felt sure I could handle him if it came to a rundown.

"As a matter of fact, I think I could have taken him in 50 yards if I'd had to. But there wasn't anything we could do about the gas shortage. Bud Moore kept screaming at me to quit testing Marcis and draft to save gas. Just as we were talking about it, I ran out of gas completely on the backstretch.

"Check to see who led the most laps, and you'll see who was fastest." Baker led 65 laps and Marcis 35.

Baker said he could "handle Marcis pretty easily."

Marcis managed a weak chuckle at that and replied, "Oh, well, I'm glad he let me catch up then."

Marcis made up some 200 yards on Baker and passed on the 174th lap after Baker's drafting partner, Richard Petty, fell out of the race.

Could Baker have passed the man from the village of Avery's Creek, NC, in a showdown? "He would have tried," Marcis answered, "but I was leading—and it's my

Dave Marcis became the first man to win the Talladega 500 from the pole.

race track when I'm leading." He told newsmen he would have attempted to block Baker.

"I figured he would try to slingshot me on the inside on the backstretch if it came down to it. That was where he could pass me," Marcis said. "But I would have run inside and made him go outside."

The answer will never be known, and that suited Marcis just fine. "It was a lot of relief to know I could back off and take it easy," he said.

The victory marked the end of a long period of frustration for Marcis. He started Winston Cup racing in 1968, but he had never won on a superspeedway. Many a finish he watched from the pits.

"We've had a lot of bad luck," the transplanted Wisconsinite said, "but I knew that one of these days we'd get enough pieces together to stay together for 500 miles. We did it today.

"And I'm happy to win at Talladega. It's the world's fastest speedway, and as far as I'm concerned they can change that sign to make it the world's fastest and the world's finest speedway."

The track did its part to live up to its reputation as the most competitive in the world. Eight drivers swapped the lead 58 times, close to the world's record of 64 set in the 1973 Talladega 500.

A.J. Foyt, who would go on to win four Indianapolis

500s and the man most considered America's best all-around race driver, made his first start at Talladega. He led six laps but was decked by engine failure after 163 laps.

Foyt had the flu, but he said, "I was determined to run this track come hell or high water."

On four previous occasions he had been scheduled to race at Talladega, but his plans had been changed by the sicknesses of his father, mother, and daughter and a rain-out.

After the race, Dave Marcis did what thousands of fans did. He got behind the wheel of his passenger car and drove home. He arrived about midnight, went to bed and slept like a babe.

An unpretentious man, Marcis found nothing inordinate about driving himself home after a harrying day on the high banks. "A friend from Wisconsin, a man who used to sponsor my car years ago, was with me, but I drove," he said.

The neighbors strung the streets with "Dave Marcis for President" signs, but the hero of Avery's Creek got up and went to his shop the next day and worked on the Sportsman car he drove on short tracks near home.

1977

Everybody seemed to have an opinion on the day before the Winston 500. "This is as good a field as they've ever had here," Richard Petty said.

"I feel better than I've ever felt about any race," Neil Bonnett said, surprisingly naming himself the favorite.

"It's going to be awfully fast," Darrell Waltrip said. "It's going to be a hell of a pack running up front. This is probably the best field they've had here in several years. It's going to be a barn-burner.

"I doubt very seriously that the fastest car will win. The cars run too fast. The winner is going to have to conserve a little bit, and most of the guys who drive fast cars are not too conservative."

One item wasn't a matter of opinion. It was a cold fact. A Chevrolet had never won a Winston Cup race at Talladega. However, A.J. Foyt had put a Chevy on the pole, and the next four qualifiers were driving that marquee.

Waltrip was starting 11th in his Chevrolet, but he was excited. The Franklin, TN, driver had won the first superspeedway race of his career a month earlier, taking the Rebel 500 at Darlington with a virtuoso spurt of driving on the last green lap.

He had been running fourth when a crash brought out the caution flag with eight laps left. Waltrip shot past the other three and beat them to the stripe, and the race finished under yellow.

It was his fourth career win, but his first on a big track. "I hope I've arrived now," he said. "I know the old rule about how it takes five years to mold a winning driver. This is my fifth year. But it seems like it's taken longer than five years."

Waltrip scored his second superspeedway victory in the Winston 500. He did it by employing that most basic of racing strategies: holding his breath and putting the pedal to the metal.

An estimated 90,000 saw Waltrip hold off Cale Yarborough, Benny Parsons and Donnie Allison on a breathtaking last lap and win by 29/100ths of a second.

The final lap began with Waltrip, Allison, Yarborough and Parsons riding in that order in a bumper-to-bumper choo-choo.

In that era, many drivers believed a man's best chance to win at Talladega was to slingshot past the leader on the last lap rather than to be the leader. But Waltrip disdained any slingshot strategy, kicked it hard in the first turn, dipped low to break the draft, and pulled away, leaving the others in a brawl that saw Yarborough get sideways in the third turn and Parsons and Yarborough bumping through three and four and down the frontstretch.

Yarborough, Pearson and Allison finished in that order behind Waltrip, nearly three abreast at the stripe.

"If there had been only two cars involved it might have been different," Waltrip said of his strategy to try to hold the lead rather than get into a slingshot position. "But with four cars in it, there's too much going on back there for any one guy to slingshot by the leader.

"I first knew they couldn't get me when I came off the fourth turn. I held my breath all the way to the finish line. I didn't see anybody gaining, and there was some squirming going on back there."

The first four finishers drove Chevrolets. as the brand got a measure of revenge for past whippings.

"I'll tell you one thing," Yarborough said. "Waltrip was lucky to win and be ahead on the last lap. If there hadn't been that situation behind him he wouldn't have won it. Out of the top four cars, Waltrip's was fourth best."

When told of the remark, the witty Waltrip shot back: "Well, I guess it was a case of superior driving on my part."

Newspapers supposed it was the best race at Talladega since the track opened in 1969. On the 67th lap Buddy Baker passed Donnie Allison for the lead—which was noteworthy because it was the 31st lead change of the day, and the highest previous figure of the year had been 30, at Daytona and Rockingham.

And 121 laps still remained to be run in the Winston 500. When it was over there had been 62 lead changes among 11 drivers.

Waltrip's victory at Darlington, which came in his 74th superspeedway start, had been questioned, but he declared the Winston 500 would have been his no matter what.

"I don't think Darlington was a fluke," Waltrip said,

Darrell Waltrip celebrates his first Talladega win with champagne.

"but some way it always ends up in the newspapers that it ended under caution, and if so-and-so hadn't done this and if so-and-so hadn't done that I wouldn't have won. Well, I would have won today no matter what so-and-so did."

Yarborough, who had taken five of the season's nine races going into the Winston 500, made a mighty run at Waltrip on the last lap. He got close enough to touch him at one time—and that might have been part of the problem.

"Cale was on the outside in turn three, and the nose of his car touched the rear of mine," Waltrip said. "He probably had to get out of the gas there, and that probably helped me some more."

Said Yarborough: "Going into three, it looked like Darrell went up to get around a slower car. So I went up, and the car got sideways."

The win at Darlington not only was Waltrip's first superspeedway triumph, it was the first for his DiGard racing team.

"Everytime we do well it helps our confidence—and we're probably about the most confident bunch out there now," Waltrip said after success No. 2 at Talladega. "We've still got a lot to learn, but we're learning fast.

"This was the first race in a long time that I did not

have a problem. Everything was beautiful all day. I got out of the draft once, but caution saved us, and we caught back up."

Foyt experienced one of his most breathtaking moments in racing when he spun on the 19th lap.

"Something happened, and oil just went all over the car," he said. "I had just gotten by Buddy Baker for second when it happened. The car got sideways and then backwards.

"They were coming at me, and here I am going backwards. Did it ever scare the heck out of me! It was one of the hairiest rides I've ever had in racing. Man, it's something to be going backwards with the whole field coming at you."

Baker was bidding for a third consecutive Winston 500 victory, but his clutch failed. He did thrill the crowd with a charge from 20th starting position to the lead in 16 laps, though.

"I was on my way again," Baker said. "I could have won the thing for the third straight time. I had no trouble at all getting up front. I was handling and could pass anyone anywhere on the track."

A man by the name of James Hylton won the 1972 Talladega 500. Dick Brooks won the 1973 Talladega 500. And Skip Manning almost won the 1977 Talladega 500.

A victory by Manning would have been celebrated as a huge upset, just as Hylton's and Brooks' wins were, but the race was a few miles too long.

Manning, a little-known sophomore driver from Bogalusa, LA, was doing justice to the Talladega 500's reputation for unpredictability when his car went sour, moments before the finish.

Manning was the surprise leader with Donnie Allison's car on his bumper when a great eruption of smoke filled his racer on the 185th lap of the 188-lap event, bringing out a yellow flag and sending Manning to the pits.

The race ended under caution. Darrell Waltrip, who had relieved Allison as driver of the Hoss Ellington Chevrolet, drove the final 23 laps in the winning car, but under NASCAR rules Allison received credit for the victory.

Cale Yarborough, who had been a quarter-mile behind Waltrip and Manning before Manning's trouble, finished second. Manning was third.

"Those last few laps I just prayed nothing would happen," Manning said, "but it did. I came in thinking it was the engine, but it was only an oil line. If I had known that I could have stayed out.

"Any time you get that close it hurts. It's like giving a child a bicycle for Christmas and taking it away from him before he unwraps it."

Manning thought it best for everyone for him to duck into the pits when the smoke storm hit. "I'm not really that hungry for a win," he said. "If I had stayed with them I would be endangering their cars and lives."

What would have happened if his car had lasted and there had been a typical Talladega last-lap shoot-out? No one will ever know.

"I felt like my car was running better than Skip's," Allison said, "and I felt like our experience—mine or Darrell's either—in having been in such situations before would be to our advantage."

Said Manning: "I knew I could outrun everybody but that car. I knew I had first or second. I think it would

have gone down to the wire."

The day was unbearably hot, with the thermometer reaching 96 in humid Talladega. Allison nearly passed out and had to call for relief near the finish. Dick May was treated for dehydration. Johnny Rutherford almost suffered heat prostration after his ice water-cooled helmet conked out, and he finally just parked his racer. Fifty-two-year-old G.C. Spencer told it like it was after requiring relief: "It's just too damn hot for an old man out there."

Spencer, incidentally, turned his car over to John Utsman, who was the answer to a NASCAR trivia question. In 1973, at Bristol, Utsman relieved Benny Parsons, and the car finished first. That was the last time before the '77 Talladega 500 that a relief driver had won.

When Allison left his Hueytown, AL, home at 7:45 on the morning of the race he noticed the temperature on the bank thermometer already read 81°, and he said to himself, "It's going to be a hot afternoon."

He realized just how hot when he got sick during the race.

Some 40 laps before the finish he pitted under caution and asked for a soft drink. He was handed one just moments before servicing of his car was completed. So he had to gulp it down in four or five quick swallows.

He thought the hastily consumed drink might have triggered his problem. "I wasn't hot or anything," Allison said, "then all of a sudden I felt like I was going to pass out.

"That's the closest I'll ever come to passing out and not do it. I told Hoss he'd better find somebody. I was passing out."

A call went out for Waltrip, whose own car had failed earlier, but before he could get to Allison's pit, the green flag waved, and the race was back under full speed.

Allison told Ellington he'd do the best he could. He was delighted to see another yellow flag on the 164th lap because that gave his team the opportunity to change drivers. Allison exited the car, climbed over the pit wall, and sank to his knees while his wife Pat comforted him.

"I probably could have gone all the way if I'd had to," he said, "but if I had passed out and wrecked and hurt

Donnie Allison and Darrell Waltrip discuss matters before the '77 Talladega 500.

myself or somebody else I'd have been foolish. So I thought it was better to let somebody else have it."

Memories of losing (to Waltrip, incidentally) on the last lap of the 1977 Winston 500 pricked at Allison's mind. "I felt like I lost the race in May," he said, "and I didn't want to take a chance of crashing and losing when I thought I was capable of winning again."

Strangely, Allison didn't see the culmination of his victory. "I didn't watch the finish," he said. "I felt my car was fast enough, and I knew Darrell was capable."

It was Waltrip's second straight trip to the speedway's victory lane—though he didn't get credit for the triumph.

"I knew Donnie had a car capable of winning, and I wanted to win it for him," Waltrip said. "It feels good to be in victory lane, no matter how you get there."

The engine in Waltrip's own car failed. "Everything was working great," he said, "and then I was coming through the trioval—and silence. I couldn't believe it got quiet so quick. Silence is not golden. When it gets that quiet you know it's over.

"What the heck. I got to play winner anyway."

Just how hot was it inside a race car under that August Alabama sun? "It was two shades cooler than hell," Allison said. "I told Hoss a few minutes ago that we'd better see about getting a cool hat"—meaning a helmet with ice water circulating through it.

The victory was the first for Allison in 10 months, and he was savoring it, despite being drained by the heat.

"Hoss' car is probably the best car I ever drove," he said, "and that includes the Wood Brothers."

For once, the Wood Brothers' racer and driver David Pearson weren't in the hunt. They lasted just 37 laps.

"Everything in that thing is hot," Pearson said, looking at his parked mount. "You talk about a sweat box, that's one. I never ran good all day. Every time I would run a full lap it would heat up. I tried to let off and cool it for awhile, but the temperature wouldn't drop. I don't know which one is the hottest right now, me or that car."

The first five finishers were in Chevrolets. Buddy Baker ran sixth in a Ford that lost a head gasket late.

"What gripes me," he said, "is that tomorrow I'll read where the Chevys were the fastest thing around. I was faster than anybody out there by seven miles an hour."

For Cale Yarborough it was to be one, two, three strikes, you're home free. After Yarborough scored his first Talladega victory in the 1978 Winston 500 he said, "There were three tracks where I hadn't won. Now there are two."

The others were Pocono and Ontario. He took care of Pocono by triumphing in 1979, but he never reached victory lane at Ontario. The final NASCAR race at the California track was contested in 1980 (a championship showdown that pulled just 15,000 fans), and the financially bedeviled white elephant was sold and torn down.

Talladega Superspeedway opened in 1969 and Ontario Motor Speedway in 1970. Automotive writers oohed and aahed about Ontario, calling it a majestic, state-of-the-art track. A friend kidded Talladega father Big Bill France about all the ink being lavished on Ontario while his speedway in Alabama got cursory mention. "That must be a quarter-mile dirt track you're building," the friend joked.

But France, a sound businessman, knew that several times as much money was being spent to construct Ontario as to build Talladega. "Yeah," he said with grin, "but in a few years Talladega will still be prospering, and Ontario will be a shopping center."

It was an example of the insight that led France to place a financially sound, ultra-competitive speedway in a locale within one day's driving distance of millions of people.

And the 1978 Winston 500 was the type race that enhanced Talladega's reputation. The last lap began with Buddy Baker in front, but Yarborough moved on him coming out of the fourth turn, passed him on the frontstretch on the day's 44th lead change, and won by two car lengths.

It was a General Motors sweep. Yarborough, Baker and fourth-placer Skip Manning drove Oldsmobiles, third-placer A.J. Foyt a Buick, and fifth-placer Grant Adcox a Chevrolet. A 22-year-old driver named Bill Elliott, who finished sixth in a Mercury, was the first non-GM man.

Yarborough dedicated his slingshot victory to all mothers—but being with mom apparently cut into the crowd. The speedway had hoped for 100,000 on May 7, but the race was rained out and re-scheduled on Mother's Day,

and the crowd was estimated at only 80,000.

Before the 500 even started, Yarborough had expected a "typical Talladega finish," meaning a final-lap showdown.

"I almost knew it would be a last-lap win, as many good cars as we had for this race," the driver of Junior Johnson's Olds said.

And when it came down to exactly that, he expected to win it. "I knew if the car held together I could beat Buddy," Yarborough said. "There was no doubt about it. I think Buddy knew what was going to happen. He had been running back in the pack most of the day, and we had been outrunning him."

Yarborough passed Baker on the inside, Foyt passed Baker on the outside, and they zipped to the finish line.

Foyt was a lap down, but he said he thought he was in the lead lap.

"A.J. didn't help on the last lap," Baker said. "He broke the draft and almost stopped the car. Other than that, I don't have any gripes. We finished a race, and that's got to be good."

"There were several places I could have passed him, and I gave it a lot of thought," Yarborough explained. "I thought about the backstretch, but I felt he might have a shot back at me if I did it there. So I decided to hold off until the last turn.

"I backed off going into three and let him get three to five car lengths ahead so I could get a running start at him. Halfway through the turn I picked it back up so I'd have a real shot coming off the fourth turn."

The traffic situation influenced the Timmonsville, SC, driver's decision, too. "I had plenty of room, and the track wasn't crowded," he said. "If there had been traffic, I might have passed on the backstretch and used the traffic."

Could Yarborough have won if their situations had been reversed, if he had been in front coming out of the fourth turn?

"If I felt that, I would have been there," he said. "I needed to do exactly what I did."

Yarborough, Donnie Allison and Darrell Waltrip appeared to have the strongest cars on the track. Allison's and Waltrip's Chevrolets were in the hunt until

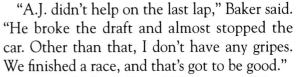

almost carry you into the wall in the second turn."

The wind wasn't all that bothered Yarborough. "One time Darrell was leading, and somebody came up in front of him, and I had to lock up my brakes at 200 miles an hour," he complained.

Elliott was in the draft with the leaders when the race ended. "I think I learned a whole bunch today," the young driver said. "We're looking forward to even better days. It sure is nice to be close to the winner when he crosses the finish line, even if I was three laps down."

Manning had mixed emotions about his fourth-place finish. "The car has never felt any better," he said. "If I hadn't gotten down a lap early in the race I think my car would have run with Cale's at the finish.

"But whenever there was a draft I moved to the back of the pack. I'm not exactly what you'd call a master of the draft. But we're going to win us one before it's over. My day is coming."

near the end when engine failure sidelined them. Donnie left after 158 laps of the 188-lapper, Darrell after 165.

Could Yarborough have beaten Allison and Waltrip if they hadn't dropped out?

"I think I had the fastest car on the track all day," Yarborough said. "We ran faster in the draft when I was leading than when the others were."

Was he most pleased to see Waltrip or Allison depart?

"Anytime a competitor goes out you feel a little better," Yarborough said, "but I think Darrell had the next strongest car."

Strong winds raked the speedway, and they bothered Yarborough. "The wind was real bad," he said. "It would

Foyt thrilled the crowd by advancing from last place to fifth in 20 laps. He had qualified second, but his microphone wire came loose on a pace lap, and he had to duck into the pits to hook it up. "If I had known that I'd have to go to the rear—I lost 39 places—I'd have stopped and fixed the thing right there on the track."

Foyt groused: "I never heard of having to go to the back of the pack before the race was even given the green flag."

Foyt also thought he finished in the lead lap instead of a lap down. "I think they've got to get the scoring straightened out here," he said.

The Talladega 500's reputation as the world's most unpredictable race—and probably the world's most unpredictable sports event—continued when Lennie Pond won in 1978.

It was the 10th Talladega 500, and Pond was the 10th different winner. For five of them, including Pond, it was their first superspeedway victory.

Pond joined Richard Brickhouse, James Hylton, Dick Brooks and Dave Marcis on the roster of those recording their first superspeedway win in the Talladega 500.

Pond hoped the tradition would end there, for only Marcis had ever won another one. It didn't. Neither Pond, Brickhouse, Hylton or Brooks ever won another Winston Cup event of any kind after their Talladega successes.

Pond won in style. An estimated 75,000 fans saw him average 174.700 miles an hour, a record for any 500-mile automobile race. The caution flag waved for just 19 laps, and the drivers, hooked up in the draft, turned some laps at more than 200 miles an hour.

There were 67 lead changes, an official world's record. Those were counted at the start-finish line. Unofficially, there were 106 all over the track.

"It was the greatest race in the history of racing," the track's general manager, Don Naman, ventured, and few would have disputed that estimation.

The 67 lead changes exceeded the record of 63 set in the 1973 Talladega 500. The 174.700 miles an hour broke Buddy Baker's world record of 169.887 set in the 1976 Winston 500.

Pond was asked if the victory carried extra meaning since it came in the fastest and most competitive 500 ever. "It does now that it's over," he said. "It will always mean a lot to me. But just to win at the fastest race track in the world... And we didn't fall into it. That makes me feel a lot better than falling into it."

Indeed, he didn't fall into anything. The Ettrick, VA, driver ran with the leaders all day. He led nine times for 22 laps and was a regular in the awesome drafts that fronted the race all day.

Donnie Allison, Cale Yarborough and Benny Parsons trailed Pond in that order as Oldsmobiles captured the first four positions. David Pearson's Mercury was fifth, a lap behind.

It was the 14th victory in 19 events for General Motors' cars. For the first time in years, a Chrysler product did not win a Winston Cup race. In fact, after the Talladega 500, Richard Petty traded in his Dodge Magnum for a Chevrolet Monte Carlo. It was the last competitive Dodge in the league.

The bulky Magnum simply wasn't suited for racing. "You could wear a cowboy hat in this thing, and it wouldn't touch the top of the car," Neil Bonnett explained.

It was a sentimental moment for Petty's fans, for the bulk of his career had been spent in Chrysler products. "Even if we don't win a race the rest of the year, we'll have the equipment that the people who are winning races have," Petty said.

It was the end of an era; Petty never drove another Chrysler product.

Swirling about Pond's helmet were rumors that he wouldn't be the driver of Harry Ranier's cars in 1979 (Buddy Baker was), and in the post-race press conference Pond said, "How about let's have a happy day for a change and forget that for awhile."

Herb Nab, the crew chief, had won many races, but this one was special. "This is the greatest feeling I've ever had in my life," he said. "Me and Waddell Wilson and Harry and Lennie put this team together, and that's why it means so much to me. It's different when you just work for somebody else that already has a team."

As one newspaper said, the final 16 laps "contained enough drama to rival the Alabama Shakespeare Festival at nearby Anniston."

Pond, Allison, Yarborough and Parsons were running bumper to bumper, each facing one more pit stop. It appeared that the man with the fastest filling station work might win the race.

Allison pitted for 8.5 seconds on the 172nd lap of the 188-lap race. Parsons took 6.5 seconds on lap 176, Yarborough 5.0 seconds on lap 177. None got tires, only fuel.

Now the spotlight was on Pond's crew. But it never had to perform under the green flag. J.D. McDuffie's car

Waltrip, Yarborough, Parsons and Petty lead the field.

stalled on the track, and the caution flag waved on lap 180.

Pond pitted and took on four new tires for top traction. Allison got two tires. Parsons chose to stay on the track and protect the lead.

Yarborough pitted for four tires, but the green flag came out on lap 183, and Yarborough pulled onto the track some 500 yards behind the front runners. The man who had led 79 laps was hopelessly behind.

The final green segment began with Parsons leading Pond, Allison and Yarborough in that order. Pond took the lead on the 184th lap and would hold it the rest of the way.

A tire blew on Bill Elliott's car, and that scattered rubber and sheet metal, including a spoiler, onto the frontstretch dogleg. The leaders ran through the debris on the 187th lap.

Parsons' fender got slammed against a tire, and he had to slow to a crawl, with no chance of victory.

Allison's windshield got smashed, apparently causing him to lift his accelerator foot for a split second and lose momentum for the final rundown.

He made a move on Pond on the outside in the final

150 yards but couldn't catch him, and Pond won by two car lengths.

"I had a chance until that tire blew," Allison said. "I'm just disgusted and glad it's over."

"I hit that spoiler, and the fender jammed up against the tire," Parsons said. "The Good Lord must have been with me though, because my tire could have gone at any time."

For a moment, Pond wondered if his Cinderella victory would evaporate in the final seconds. "I saw that stuff on the track and knew I just had to keep it wide open and hope it didn't hurt anything," he said. "I really felt it hit the car hard the first time I went through it, but if I hit any of it the second time I didn't feel it."

Petty led four times in his Dodge swan song. He finished seventh, two laps behind.

"The car ran real well today," he said. "We were up there among the leaders for awhile. But we ran out of gas and lost a lap, got out of the draft and finally got behind. Those Oldsmobiles were going."

Remember the old movie, "God Is My Co-Pilot?" The sequel played at Talladega in '79. Bobby Allison's racer negotiated a 17-car crash showroom clean, and the Hueytown, AL, driver won his second event at the world's biggest speedway.

"The Good Lord drove that car for me," Allison said. "I had a nice channel right through the middle of it. A couple of cars just went up and out of my way, and a couple went down and out of my way."

The melee started at the beginning of the fifth lap when "something razor sharp" cut leader Buddy Baker's right rear tire, and his car swerved.

"It was like being in the tunnel at a stadium with the Alabama football team running at you," said Baker, who had started on the outside of the front row.

It was amazing that no one was seriously injured, although Cale Yarborough did get a scare. After he climbed out of his car, D.K. Ulrich's racer hit him, pinning his legs against Dave Marcis' tire.

"He thought his legs were cut off," Dr. J.L. Hardwick of the speedway care center said. "His legs were numb, and then he thought maybe they were paralyzed. As time went by he began to get some feeling back. He's all right." Hardwick kept Yarborough in the care center an hour and a half.

"It was the (most scared) I've ever ever been," admitted Yarborough, who asked Marcis to look and see whether his legs were cut off. "If it had been metal to metal it probably would have been all over. It probably would have cut my legs off."

The wreck was reminiscent of the 21-car crash in the 1973 Winston 500 that left David Pearson with an easy victory.

"All of a sudden my car took off for the wall," said Baker, who was driving for the Harry Ranier team that fielded Lennie Pond's winning racer in the 1978 Talladega 500.

"All I know is that it's an awful feeling when the steering wheel on your car doesn't mean anything. The only thing that's wrong with me is that my right arm is a little sore. It kinda felt like somebody hit me in the arm with a baseball bat. I'm just glad nobody was hurt. Something

razor sharp cut my tire."

A crowd estimated at 100,000 saw Allison and his Hueytown neighbor Neil Bonnett drive through the crash, their cars unscathed, and by the 60th circuit they were a lap ahead of everyone else.

Hueytown drivers were running 1-2-3, with Bonnett leading Bobby Allison and Donnie Allison, when Donnie's engine blew on the 82nd lap.

Bonnett, in his first start as the replacement for Pearson in the Wood Brothers Mercury, clearly had the fastest car, and he was 15 seconds ahead of Bobby Allison's Bud Moore Ford when his engine blew on the 149th lap of the 188-lapper. The race was handed to Bobby, who finished a lap ahead of runner-up Darrell Waltrip, whose car that was battered in the big wreck.

"He had a better than 50 percent chance of winning even if we had drafted to the end," Bobby said of Bonnett. "I would have had to have everything going for me."

The lead pack had been clocked at 203 miles an hour on the lap before the massive crash. Bobby admitted he was somewhat conservative in the early going at Talladega. "You can't win the race unless you get to the last mile," he said.

He won because he got to the last mile and Bonnett didn't.

Bonnett and Waltrip, who was a lap down, hooked up in a draft and left Bobby. "They motored away from me," he said, "but I could see they were turning a lot of rpms. I just sat there and let my car run cool. But I didn't figure Neil would blow."

Neil did blow, and that left Waltrip, who tried to unlap himself but couldn't. "I felt I could beat Darrell to the line under any circumstances with his Oldsmobile beaten up like that from the wreck," Bobby said. "We had 'em out-streamlined for a change."

What are a driver's thoughts after he escapes a 17-car wreck?

"You hate to see it, of course, and you're apprehensive about anybody getting hurt," Bobby said, "but after I came around I saw everybody was okay. Well, one was on a stretcher, but he didn't appear badly hurt. Once you get past two or three laps of looking over the mess you have

Bobby Allison rides the high road in the '79 Winston 500.

to go on to business as usual."

Brother Donnie Allison charged from 21st place to smell the leaders' exhaust, but the wreck banged up his car and cost him a lap, and his engine eventually blew.

"All I saw in that wreck was cars everywhere," he said. "I was trying to keep from getting run over in that wreck. I tore a clutch up, and my car was vibrating. Before the wreck I was flying. I know one thing: I caught the front pack right at the beginning of the race."

The accident ended the hopes of young Tighe Scott, who had qualified fifth.

"All I saw was a bunch of smoke," Scott said. "I was in the trioval and saw a bunch of smoke down in the first turn. There was so much smoke down there you couldn't see anything. Everything just happened so quick. This is the farthest up we've started, and I was really looking forward to today."

Buddy Arrington, who was a surprising fourth in qualifying, escaped the crash and finished third, his highest spot in more than 300 Winston Cup races.

"I gave it the gas all day, how about that?" said Arrington. "It was the best race I ever drove.

"They were a little too wild for me to start with, and I needed to finish the race to make some money, so I was being cautious at first.

"I knew that I could run with them all along. The car, crew, everything was just perfect. It was really an unreal day. I'm as happy as if I had won."

Arrington drove a Dodge he bought from Richard Petty, and Petty spent much of the afternoon with his Oldsmobile on Arrington's rear bumper.

"What I need is a Dodge," joked Petty, who had left the Chrysler camp after the 1978 Talladega 500. "That wreck knocked my front end out a little bit, and I couldn't run a lick. I drafted Buddy all day, and he really helped me along."

For a pre-race story, a newspaper interviewed 10 backmarkers as to who they thought would win the Winston 500. Five picked Bonnett, none picked Bobby Allison. Bonnett's car was so strong that it led 121 laps. Bobby's led 58 laps, and no one else was in double figures. There were only 20 lead changes.

Bobby was beaming as the sun sank below the rim of the speedway. "It's been a big weekend for me," he said. "My 18-year-old son Davey drove at Birmingham International Raceway last night and won his first race."

1979

When the Talladega 500 rolled off, there were two Pettys in the starting field of a Winston Cup race for the first time since 1964.

Kyle Petty's debut was historic but uneventful. The grandson and son of champions started 18th and finished ninth, seven laps behind. "He qualified, ran a 500-miler and finished," said dad Richard. "I guess he's on his way to a racing career."

It was a race that wasn't cast from the well-worn Talladega mold. There was no "typical Talladega finish." Darrell Waltrip ran away with the thing. He had a lap on the field with 100 miles to go, and the only reason runner-up David Pearson finished on the lead circuit was because Waltrip allowed him to unlap himself on the final go-round. Waltrip led 102 of the 188 laps.

The patriarch of stock car racing's first family, Lee Petty, won 54 races and three Winston Cup championships before a terrible crash at Daytona in 1961 ended his career.

His son, Richard, began racing in 1958 and won 200 races and seven Winston Cup titles, both records, before he retired after the 1992 season.

Richard's brother Maurice had a brief and winless career as a Winston Cup driver before giving it up to devote all his time to the mechanical side. He and Richard drove against each other a few times, and they were the last Petty driving duo, in 1964, before Kyle and Richard raced together at Talladega.

Kyle, a star high school quarterback who could have gone to college on a football scholarship, was more interested in following in the tire prints of his father and grandfather.

Kyle began working in the Petty shops in 1978. "He needs to work on the car," Richard said. "He's got to understand everything about the car before he ever gets in and starts driving it. He goes to school a half day and then works in the shop. He tells me he definitely wants to try driving a race car. Where he goes is anybody's guess."

Lee didn't permit Richard to drive a racer until he was 21, and Richard had said Kyle couldn't race until he was 21, however, Richard relented and fielded one of his old Dodge Magnums for his 18-year-old son in the 1979 ARCA 200 at Daytona. Richard had switched from

Dodge to Chevrolet after the 1978 Talladega 500, and the car was collecting dust.

Some questioned the wisdom of a driver beginning his career on the 2.5-mile Daytona International Speedway. "The trend today is toward the superspeedways," Richard explained. "If he did well on the short tracks he'd have to unlearn everything he learned when he finally came to a big track. If he can't cut it here, there's no sense in messing around on the short tracks."

When asked the morning of the ARCA 200 if he felt pressure, Kyle replied with typical Petty aplomb: "If it's there I don't feel it. I'm not the favorite. I know I probably won't win the race."

But he did win it. He charged from his No. 2 starting position to lead most of the way. John Rezek's slingshot attempt on the last lap failed, and Kyle Petty, incredibly, won by two lengths.

His first Winston Cup effort came at Charlotte in May, but he crashed twice and didn't get to attempt qualifying for the World 600. Next up was Daytona, where he crashed during qualifying for the Firecracker 400. He spent the Fourth of July working in Richard's crew instead of driving.

But he made the field and completed the show at Talladega, and a Winston Cup career was born.

Said Kyle when it was over: "My goal was just to finish the race. I wasn't even thinking about finishing in the top 10. Where did I finish, anyway? I was a little cautious about drafting, and when the faster cars would come up on me I wanted to let them by so they could do their thing."

A crowd estimated at 80,000 saw Waltrip dominate. With his sixth victory of the season the Franklin, TN, driver surpassed his money winnings for all of 1978 and equaled his victory total of that year.

When a writer reminded him that he said before the season he'd be happy to match 1978's accomplishments, the driver of the DiGard Chevrolet smiled and answered, "If I had known we were going to have this kind of year, I wouldn't have said that."

With numerous top dogs experiencing difficulties, the

Darrell Waltrip drove "Bertha" to victory in the '79 Talladega 500.

first 20 read like a who's not who of racing.

Past Waltrip and Pearson, only Richard Petty, who finished fourth, was a true big name in the top 20.

Ricky Rudd ran third, Sportsman driver Jody Ridley fifth, Tighe Scott sixth, Harry Gant seventh, Buddy Arrington eighth, Kyle Petty ninth and Richard Childress 10th.

Neil Bonnett, the pole sitter, led 40 of the 77 laps he lasted, but his engine failed.

Cale Yarborough fought Waltrip mightily after Bonnett's exit and led 14 laps, but the rear end of his car failed, and he got in only 138 laps.

When Benny Parsons made a long pit stop with 100 laps to go, Waltrip completed his lapping of the field. He knew then that "all I had to do was finish. I didn't want to make any foolish mistakes.

"I wanted to slow down, but I knew all it would take would be a caution flag and the others would be back up with me, so I kept driving my race. From all indications of the gauges, I could have driven that fast all day."

It was Pearson's first start since he split with the Wood Brothers team in April. He was substituting for the injured Dale Earnhardt in Rod Osterlund's car. He was worthy opposition on the track, but his Oldsmobile had a clutch problem, and he lost valuable time creeping away from his pit stops. A malfunctioning radio also hampered his effort.

"Everybody was congratulating me for second," Pearson said. "It's kinda funny to be patted on the back for losing.

"We didn't have radio contact all day, and the clutch went out early. With a radio and clutch, I think we would have won the race. We had no chance to consider strategy, and it's tough to run a superspeedway these days without radio contact."

Waltrip became the 11th different winner in 11 Talladega 500s as one of the most amazing streaks in sports continued.

"It's different from the May race in that it's so terribly hot, and the heat takes the toll of man and machine," Waltrip reasoned. "For instance, today, with about 100 miles to go, five or six good cars had mechanical problems at the same time."

The speedway was sporting a $600,000 facial for the Winston 500, and the racing teams were making eyes at her.

The 2.66-mile facility had been paved for the first time since it opened in 1969, and speed and improved handling became the name of the game in the days leading up to the race.

"It will be the fastest race they've ever had here," said Harry Hyde, crew chief for Tighe Scott.

"The lead change total might just go out of sight," Neil Bonnett figured.

"It will be one of the toughest races you ever saw," Cale Yarborough predicted.

Bonnett found the new surface a delight. "I ran over 200 miles an hour in the draft Friday, and it was so comfortable it scares you. There were 20 in the lead draft here last year, but there will be 25 or 30 this time."

Buddy Baker agreed that the draft would be more crowded. "It's not as hard to keep up," he said. "Last year my hair was standing on end, but now it's not that hard to keep control of the car."

Bonnett continued: "The Oldsmobiles were on the borderline in handling here, but now everybody's handling again. To run a real good lap drafting you need to run directly behind a guy. Before, you couldn't do that. Now you can run behind a guy and not vary four to six inches. That should pick the speed up."

The fastest field in the track's history at that time started the race. David Pearson won the pole with a run of 197.704 as the first 27 in the field of 42 exceeded 190.

"If you see someone who says this isn't going to be a hell of a race, I'd like to know who it is," Hyde demanded.

Harry had it pegged. It was a great race. There were 40 lead changes among a dozen drivers, and Buddy Baker and Dale Earnhardt finished side by side, with Baker winning by three or four feet.

Perhaps half the estimated 90,000 to 100,000 spectators didn't know who won when the drivers crossed the finish line at 200 miles an hour, but Baker knew.

"You learn to look out of the side of your face," the driver of the Ranier Racing Oldsmobile said. "When we reached the flagstand I looked over and the front of his car was back on my door handle. We were half a car length ahead."

It was a heart-attack ending to an event best described by that motorsports cliché, a "typical Talladega race."

The final chapter of the drama began on lap 153 of the 188-lap contest. Baker and Earnhardt, who were far out front, pitted under green. Dale's crew put on right-side tires in 14.8 seconds. Baker's opted for four tires, and his stop took 31.2 seconds.

When Buddy returned to the track, he was 18 seconds behind—at about a football field a second.

The Charlotte driver relentlessly began to reel in Earnhardt. Would he catch him or would he run out of laps?

Baker reached Earnhardt's bumper on the first turn of the 186th lap then shot by him on the backstretch.

Earnhardt made a move on Baker on the backstretch of the last lap, but a lapped car forced him back into line.

Earnhardt started another bid for victory in the frontstretch dogleg, 400 yards from the finish line. He dipped low, and Baker didn't block the track. They crossed the stripe side by side.

"This stuff of cutting people off on the track is okay, but eventually somebody is going to put you to the test," Baker said of his decision not to attempt to block Earnhardt. "I gave him racing room."

"Baker just overpowered us at the end," Earnhardt said. "He had a little more horsepower. My car was working as well as his, but I just didn't have enough to get back around him after he passed me. I had it wide open all the way around."

Baker considered riding behind Earnhardt and then attempting a slingshot maneuver on the last lap. "But I have a tremendous amount of confidence in this race car," he said. "I've never had a car that performed like this one. I just decided to go ahead and pass him and hope that was the right decision."

Baker's crew chief, Waddell Wilson, knew changing four tires during the pivotal stop would be costly—but he also knew changing just two could be more costly. "I've

Baker claims his fourth Talladega triumph.

He could talk to them, but he couldn't hear them. But when he saw his fans waving their caps with a "charge" motion he knew he was gaining on Earnhardt.

"I knew then that man was in trouble if we had enough laps to go," Baker said. "I could see him coming back to me. I just hoped it wouldn't take too long."

"If we had only had a few more seconds lead we might have won it," Earnhardt iffed.

Baker looked pale when he pulled into victory lane. "I was fine until they dropped the checkered flag," he said. "Then I got sick. I guess it was just the strain."

Baker, who led for 60 laps, thus became the only man to win four races at Talladega. One reporter asked him if winning there was becoming easier. Baker obviously considered that the question of the day. "If it gets any easier I think I'll have a nervous breakdown," he said. "I don't think they'll ever run one any closer than this one."

The predicted drafts of 25 to 30 cars didn't materialize, but the frontrunners charged out in a 10-car bunch instead.

At halfway, Cale Yarborough, Earnhardt, Baker, Pearson, Benny Parsons, Lennie Pond, Bonnett and Scott were bumper to bumper.

Bonnett's engine failed after 99 laps, and green-flag pit stops about two-thirds of the way spread out the leaders, leaving Yarborough 150 yards ahead of Earnhardt, Baker and Benny Parsons, Pearson far behind them, Pond way behind Pearson and Scott far behind Pond. Within a few laps, Parsons had to make an unscheduled stop, and Baker and Earnhardt drove away from Yarborough, whose engine was skipping, and it was a two-car race, finally decided by the margin of three or four feet.

never been on a race car where the driver got hurt," Wilson explained. "I won't gamble with a driver's life. I thought I'd change four tires even if it cost us the race."

Did that mean Earnhardt was in jeopardy with just two new tires?

"We don't concern ourselves with what other teams do," Baker replied, heading off that line of questioning.

Suppose the decision had been Baker's? Would he have taken on four tires?

"Thank God they don't leave it to me," Buddy said. "I wouldn't have any tires on it."

He added: "It's hard to see the guy you've been racing with pull out of the pits and know they're just jacking up the left side of our car. But Waddell calls the shots, and I knew we had a good car, one I had confidence in."

Baker's radio contact with his crewmen malfunctioned.

A driver is about to lay his life on the line at 200 miles an hour. He is as tense as a young preacher before his first sermon, right?

There are more butterflies in his stomach than in a petunia patch, right?

Well, that wasn't exactly the case with Neil Bonnett before the Talladega 500.

The Hueytown, AL, driver and his Wood Brothers Mercury team made $35,175 for their victory, but their net was $35,075.

"I was sitting in a lounge chair in the infield building, and I went to sleep and missed the driver's meeting before the race," Bonnett admitted. "I woke up and they told me NASCAR had fined me $100 for missing it. So I went back to sleep.

"I woke up later and heard the man on the PA introducing the drivers at the start-finish line. He said, 'Starting in 18th place...' and I knew I'd better get over there because it was only 16 places up to me."

Bonnett was just as cool on the last lap. He lost the lead to Dale Earnhardt on the backstretch but took it back in the fourth turn and won a thriller.

"I enjoyed myself out there today," the loosey-goosey Bonnett commented. "I sat out there and said, 'I've got 'em today.' Of course, I'm sure Cale and Dale were saying the same thing."

For the estimated 65,000 on the grounds, the suspense wasn't over when Bonnett crossed the line, a winner by six lengths. Earnhardt and Yarborough were side by side in a photo finish. Yarborough got second and Earnhardt third with Benny Parsons on their bumpers. Harry Gant ran fifth, the only other driver on the lead lap.

Bonnett's payoff included a $7,500 bonus for becoming the 12th different winner in 12 Talladega 500s. That tied a Winston Cup record. The Western North Carolina 500, contested at Asheville-Weaverville Speedway (1958-69), also had a dozen different winners in a row.

The victory lifted Bonnett's spirits; his past record at his home track had been incredibly bad. His previous finishing positions at Talladega had been 39,45,35,38,39,25,28,8,39,34,17 and 27.

"I've been busting my can trying to win in my back-

yard," Bonnett said. "I've got a lot of friends out there watching me."

Bonnett hadn't won since Nov. 4, 1979, until he captured the Coca-Cola 500 at Pocono on July 27. His Talladega victory made it two in a row.

"Leonard Wood is plenty capable of making a car run like gangbusters every week," Bonnett said. "The only governor is having the engine parts that will last. Now we've been able to get them."

The team kept its poise through a rash of non-finishes. "When you're continually breaking valve springs and you've got the best parts you can get, there's no need to get mad at each other," Bonnett said.

Bonnett's drought-breaking victory at Pocono was a thriller. He passed Buddy Baker with four laps to go and won by half a second. Then there was the heart-stopper at Talladega.

"People ask me why I've got gray hair," the 34-year-old Bonnett said after the Talladega victory. "They ought to come out and watch one of these things, then they'd know. I'd like one day to win an easy race." But then he reconsidered and said, "No, I wouldn't either. These are more memorable."

Bonnett and Yarborough had vamoosed from the rest of the field, but a caution flag on the 178th lap of the 188-lap race created a four-car finish. When the green waved on 182 it was Yarborough, Bonnett, Earnhardt, Gant and Parsons in a choo-choo.

Earnhardt and Bonnett drafted by Yarborough on 184, and Bonnett passed Earnhardt on 185.

Bonnett, Earnhardt, Yarborough and Parsons started the last lap in that order, glued together.

Earnhardt went low and nosed ahead of Bonnett on the backstretch, but he couldn't get all the way around and Bonnett took him on the outside in the last turn. Then Yarborough edged Earnhardt for second.

The first eight laps were run under caution to dry the track after a shower. That gave Richard Petty plenty of time to turn his car over to Joe Millikan. Petty had suffered a neck injury in a crash at Pocono and planned only to start the race to receive his points.

It was a day of long lead drafts, as long as 13 cars, but

Neil Bonnett, driving for Wood Brothers, wins the '80 Talladega 500.

the usual attrition reduced the list of contenders to four at the end.

Baker, the pole sitter, fell out on the 61st lap after he had led practically all the way. He was bidding for a sweep of Talladega's 1980 Winston Cup races.

"I don't really know what happened," Baker said. "We cracked a cylinder head, or maybe it was the ignition. It just quit on the backstretch. If I ever had an advantage on the field it was today."

Despite his early exit, Baker led the most laps, 56. Bonnett led 52. There were 36 lead changes among 11 drivers.

Gant hinted he might be about to polish up the tradition of underdogs winning the Talladega 500, but a part of his windshield blew out, and his car wasn't aerodynamically sound enough to contend at the end.

Surprisingly strong, to the delight of Alabama fans, was Hueytown's Donnie Allison, who led the 500. Allison recently had joined a team owned by coal-mining magnate Ken Childers. The team had never won a Winston Cup event.

But a tire blew and a piece of rubber severed Donnie's oil line, sending him to the garage. "That's the best our team has run," he said. "I feel good about the way we ran, but then some freak thing like this happens. Of course, anything can happen to me."

As Bonnett said, he had fun. But a fellow didn't have to win to have fun. Just finishing the race was a kick for country-western singer Marty Robbins, who got 13th place, 15 laps behind Bonnett.

"About the last 10 laps I was soaking wet, and my ribs were hurting, and my transmission was going," Robbins explained, "but I said I was going to finish even if I had to finish in low gear.

"I just race to have fun, and man, did I have fun today."

The 1980 Winston Cup season was the last for full-sized cars. NASCAR ruled that, effective in 1981 the racers would be limited to a wheelbase of 110 inches, reduced from 115.

For five years, NASCAR pondered the possibility of downsizing Winston Cup racers. "Eventually we will have to follow Detroit's trend," Bill France Jr., the president, said. And the shift in Detroit was toward smaller passenger cars.

Before the 1981 season, NASCAR relegated the 115-inch wheelbase racers to history and set the new standard at 110.

For the teams, this meant a change from reliable, bulky cars to machines about which questions fluttered like butterflies.

It was a shaky time for stock car racing. "The car is not handling well at all," Bobby Allison said after he and Darrell Waltrip ran tests at Daytona in 1980. "After two days of testing, all we did was get the car from horrible to bad. I had hoped to do some drafting with Darrell, but right now I don't even want the seagulls out there with me."

The small cars were as fast as the big ones, but they had "poor handling characteristics," Waltrip said.

Dale Earnhardt's team tested later, and he said, "I was as nervous as hell during those tests. The cars aren't stable enough to run in a pack."

"This is a whole new ball game," Richard Petty said.

In one of the qualifying races for the Daytona 500, John Anderson's car spun—and it seemed to take off like an airplane, flying a short distance. Then Connie Saylor got in trouble, and his car lifted in the air, nose down, tail up.

Drivers and crewmen gathered in the drivers' lounge to watch TV replays. No one could recall seeing race cars make similar motions.

They looked like "cardboard boxes blowing in the wind," Benny Parsons said. "It beats anything I've ever seen."

NASCAR increased the allowable spoiler area on the cars and worked with the teams to keep them on the ground, but naturally there was apprehension when the tour arrived at Talladega, Daytona's super-fast sister track.

There was a collective sigh of relief when there appeared to be no handling crisis in the Winston 500. NASCAR was delighted to hear Bobby Allison, the winner, say, "My car handled like a charm and ran like a charm all day."

Still, the effort to keep the race cars from flying would be an ongoing battle over the years.

The Winston 500 was another great Talladega race—once they got the caution flag back in its sheath.

There were 44 lead changes among 10 drivers. Allison passed Buddy Baker entering the third turn of the final lap and held off a squadron that included Baker, Waltrip and Ricky Rudd. Those three finished in that order, side by side, scant feet off Allison's rear bumper.

Or they would have been on his rear bumper if he had had one. It was a casualty early in the 500, when the race resembled a filmmaker's re-creation of World War II.

A 10-car crash on the second lap ended the fray for Bill Elliott, Petty, Joe Millikan, Saylor, Parsons, Stan Barrett and Harry Gant. Actor Burt Reynolds saw both of his machines, driven by Barrett and Gant sidelined before he had time to get comfortable in his seat.

The wreck wasn't as serious as the 21-car crash of 1973 or the 17-car smashup of 1979, but it was hardly a fender-bender.

"Darrell Waltrip caught me in the front end and turned me into Rick Wilson," said Gant, explaining the beginning of the accident. "I think Darrell just tried to cut back in front of me too quick and just pinched me off.

"I don't know how many times I got hit, but I remembered getting hit once when I was going across the track, and then I got hit another time when I was down on the apron. I know I gave the wall one heck of a lick.

"When I hit the wall my hood came flying off, and that really got exciting."

Said Waltrip: "We went into the third turn three wide, with me up high. I dropped down in front of Harry, and I guess we might have touched. It certainly wasn't intentional."

Gant's teammate, Barrett, counted his chickens before his eggs got scrambled. "I thought I had made it through all the mess," he said, "and then one of the black cars came down — I think it was Connie Saylor—and I hit him. Before that I had been saying to myself, 'I've made it through all of this.' But then, wham! I couldn't believe

Pontiac's safety car paces the field before the start of the Winston 500.

what happened."

A crowd estimated at 100,000 saw the caution wave four times in the first 37 laps. After 40 laps, the average speed was 92.259 miles an hour, hardly an indication that it would be settled in a sizzling 199-mph finish.

When Allison pitted during the third caution for his crew to rip off his dragging rear bumper and tape his broken windshield, there was hardly an indication, either, that he would be the winner.

Allison drove his Harry Ranier Racing Buick from a lap down to win. He pitted under green on lap 135 when he felt a tire going down. He couldn't tell which one it was, so his crew changed all four, and he lost a lap.

But debris on the track brought out another yellow on lap 156, and Allison beat Baker back to the line and made up the lap.

With 28 laps to go, the green flag waved a four-car duel into session. Allison, Baker, Waltrip and Rudd kicked the lead around, and Baker was in front when the final lap began. But Allison went low at the end of the backstretch, got under Baker and held the trio off the rest of the way.

Allison had difficulty finding anyone to draft with—at least until the stretch, when Waltrip tucked in behind the Hueytown, AL, driver and foiled Baker's chance for a run at the leader.

"My car handled like a charm and ran like a charm all day," Allison said. "It was stronger than anyone else's, but I couldn't get anybody to line up behind me. They kept lining up behind somebody else and pushing them by me. But Darrell did come in behind me at the end, and I appreciated him helping me win."

Baker didn't appreciate it. "I thought I had a good shot at Bobby, and then he jammed on his brakes, and I had to go high," Buddy said. "Then Darrell stuck his nose under me, even though it was all he could do to hang on. When Darrell drove up, it didn't help me a bit. I had to go to racing Darrell, and I knew it was all over then. It was all I could do to hang on for second. I knew Darrell couldn't win, but I had a good shot."

"I'll assure you there were no brake shoes involved at all," Allison said.

The question was, who would win the Talladega 500, Darrell Waltrip or Terry Labonte? The answer was Ron Bouchard.

The rookie from Fitchburg, MA, was in third place when the trio reached the frontstretch dogleg on the last lap, but when they crossed the finish line three abreast, he had edged Waltrip by a foot or two, and Waltrip had nosed out Labonte by a similar margin.

The fans weren't the only ones who were stunned.

"Terry and I got to racing each other and completely forgot ol' Ron Bouchard," Waltrip said. "Where did he come from, anyway?"

"I thought I had Darrell right where I wanted him for the last lap," Labonte said. "I was running right ahead of him, going through the dogleg, and then Bouchard snuck under us at the flag. Darrell and I were so busy racing each other that he just slipped by."

It was easy to forget Bouchard. Like James Hylton and Dick Brooks before him, he was a most unlikely winner of the Talladega 500.

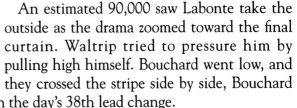

When the Winston Cup season opened, the 32-year-old Bouchard was up in Massachusetts and Connecticut, driving a Modified racer on short tracks.

Bob Johnson, crew chief of the Race Hill Farm team in Madison, CT, was fielding a Winston Cup car for Harry Gant and gritting his teeth. When he embarked on the cornpone and grits circuit a couple of years before, all the Connecticut Yankee heard was that he was nuts, that he couldn't beat those Southerners. "They put their pants on just like I do, one leg at a time," he declared, vowing that he would win a Winston Cup race.

But he hadn't won, and in March, Gant quit to drive for another team.

Johnson had had difficulty getting dialed in with Gant. He wanted a driver he had worked with before, so he summoned Bouchard, who had driven his Modifieds in previous years but who had never been in a big league racer.

In his first 10 Winston Cup starts, Bouchard failed to crack the top five. One of the 10 was the Winston 500, in which he drove just 372 miles, unnoticed, before his engine failed.

"But that race helped us here today," Bouchard said after magic tapped his shoulder in the Talladega 500. "I

knew more about what the car needed to run Talladega, and it helped me as a driver to have been here before."

Bouchard became the 13th different winner in 13 Talladega 500s, a Winston Cup record.

The $38,805 he earned for his victory was just $400 short of his total winnings in his 10 previous Winston Cup races.

Perhaps he used some of it to buy his father a television set. Back home in Fitchburg, Pop was watching the final few laps of the Talladega 500, but when the picture disappeared he missed what was perhaps the greatest finish in automobile racing history.

"I called my dad as soon as I got a chance," Ron said a couple of hours after the race. "He said he was beating on the television set, and he finally just threw it on the floor."

An estimated 90,000 saw Labonte take the outside as the drama zoomed toward the final curtain. Waltrip tried to pressure him by pulling high himself. Bouchard went low, and they crossed the stripe side by side, Bouchard winning on the day's 38th lead change.

"I knew I had to do the opposite of whatever they did," Bouchard said. "I waited until Terry made his move because he was second. When he moved to the top and Darrell moved out with him, I got a good draft or something and went right by them. Going high was the route I wanted because I had been running well up high. I was hoping Terry would go low, but he didn't. It turned out okay, though."

Noted Waltrip: "Bouchard went by me and Terry like we were tied to a tree."

"I glanced over as we crossed the finish line three abreast, and I thought I had beaten Darrell by a foot, but I didn't know," Bouchard said. "I tried to call the crew, but the radio wouldn't work. Then I looked up at the scoreboard and saw my number in first place."

The frustration of having been unable to beat the Rebels tempered Johnson's reaction. "The guys in the crew were going wild," he said, "but I told them, 'Don't get so excited. Let's be sure we won it first'."

"We ran fast right off the trailer," Bouchard said, "and in practice Saturday we were basically as fast as any of

Ron Bouchard edges Waltrip (11) and Labonte (44) in a photo finish.

them. I expected a good finish."

So did the handsome divorcee's girlfriend. "You know," she said over breakfast, "you're going to win the Talladega 500 today."

Bouchard answered: "I just might do that."

For Bouchard, winning in just his 11th Winston Cup start was the highlight of a racing career that began at 14—even earlier if you include working on race cars.

His father, a truck line owner, had short-track cars years before, and Ron worked on them as a little boy.

When he was 14 he started driving—but not his dad's racer. Pop quickly put a stop to that, and Ron had to wait until he was 16 to resume his career.

Bouchard had a coach at Talladega. "I had never really met Buddy Baker," he said. "We were next to his team in the garage, and I introduced myself and just started asking him questions.

"He told me how to drive in the draft and how to pass and when to pass. If it hadn't been for Buddy, I don't think I would have won this race."

Bobby Allison said he was the one who should have won it. He led 106 of the 188 laps and was ahead on the 181st circuit when he lost a cylinder and had to ride it

out to fifth place.

"I'm real disappointed," Allison said. "I had the strongest car on the race track until the time it counted. The car ran perfectly all day and handled perfectly all day, but we ran out of luck at the end.

"We should have been the ones to win the race. We should have been the first two-time winner of the Talladega 500."

Gant was in the battle, too, until the 177th lap, when he had to back off.

"Our luck started out rotten," he said. "First, our radio went out. Then we had a super bad vibration that slowed me down. I backed off and got out of the way because I was afraid something was going to break, and I didn't want to mess things up for the rest of them."

Another driver thinking of what might have been was Cale Yarborough, who wrecked on the 84th lap.

"Somebody blew an engine going into the first turn," he said. "Bobby Allison backed off, and I backed off, and whoever was behind me hit me. I think Bobby and I had the two fastest cars out there today."

But the victor was rookie Ron Bouchard—who never won another Winston Cup race.

Who was the first stock car driver to run a 200-mile-per-hour qualifying lap at Talladega? If you said Benny Parsons you are absolutely wrong.

Billie Harvey drove 200.642 miles an hour in August, 1981, while qualifying for the ARCA 200. But ARCA's restrictions weren't as tight as NASCAR's, and it was Parsons' run of 200.176 to win the pole for the 1982 Winston 500 that excited the public and oiled the typewriters and TV cameras.

Though Charlie Glotzbach had won the pole for the 1969 Talladega 500 at 199.466 and Buddy Baker had sped 200.447 in a test in 1970, no Winston Cup driver had ever reached 200 in qualifying until Parsons did it on April 29, 1982.

It was a dramatic episode in racing. Technology and genius and bravery tore down another barrier.

Parsons topped 200 in practice on Thursday, and someone asked the Ellerbe, NC, driver if he felt pressure to match the lap in qualifying later that day.

"No," he answered. "Fortunately, there's nothing I can mess up on this track. I just put my foot down on the floor and steer. It's a foolproof situation for me. I'm sure the team over there has a tremendous amount of pride and satisfaction in what we've accomplished. They deserve the credit."

Perhaps Parsons wouldn't have reached 200 if Baker hadn't attached a note to his Winston 500 entry blank declaring the speed was a possibility.

"I hadn't even thought about it until I read about it in the paper," Parsons said, "and my first reaction was that I didn't believe anybody could go that fast. Then I thought about running 196 at Daytona and said, 'Hey, maybe that's realistic'."

After Parsons hit 198 in practice Wednesday, Waddell Wilson, his engine builder, said, "Man, it would be nice to run 200."

The crew kept tinkering, gaining hundredths of seconds. They got to within half a mile an hour of 200 and smelled blood.

Finally, their stopwatch told them the Ranier Racing

Pontiac broke 200 in practice. Then Parsons had to do it when it counted. He did. His first qualifying lap was clocked at 200.013. Then he ran the second at 200.176.

"I saw the crowd stand up and clap, and I realized I probably had the fastest time," Parsons said. "Then the question was whether I had made 200."

Parsons isn't a guy who leaps to the podium and leads cheers when he accomplishes something. "But it really is exciting to break 200," he said. "And it probably will get bigger with time."

Sixteen months before, the downsized cars had been introduced at Daytona, and they had handled poorly and been dog-cussed. Now they were running 200 miles an hour. Where would it end?

"There's no ultimate speed," Parsons said. "People keep working year in and year out to make the cars better. Goodyear is always working to make better tires for them. People like Waddell Wilson are working to improve the engines. The chassis people are working to get them through the corners better."

Darrell Waltrip and Dale Earnhardt predicted at a press conference two days earlier that no one would run 200 in time trials.

"Dale and I were talking this morning," Waltrip commented after qualifying, "and we agreed everybody is going to say, 'That's two dumb guys'."

Parsons spoke up: "In their defense, this is unusual weather. This is the coldest it has ever been."

Thursday was an unseasonably chilly, overcast day that was made for qualifying, for breaking the 200-mph barrier.

No one else reached 200 in qualifying. Waltrip did 199.388 and Ricky Rudd 199.446, and then the speeds dropped into the 197s. The fastest field that had ever started a Winston Cup race rolled off on Sunday.

But qualifying isn't the race itself, and when Waltrip, Terry Labonte, Parsons and Kyle Petty reached the Final Four of the Winston 500, the championship went to Waltrip.

An estimated 100,000 persons saw another Talladega breath-holder, and the victor's estimation of the showdown spoke volumes about the unpredictability of the

Bill Elliott on the move in the '82 Winston.

(left) Waltrip was among the leaders all day.
(below) Joe Ruttman (75), Mark Martin (02) and Geoff Bodine (50) battle for position.

Stevie and Darrell Waltrip enjoy victory lane after the '82 Winston 500.

track: "Put us back out there and let us run 10 laps, and somebody else would win it."

The last lap began with Parsons, Waltrip, Labonte and Petty locked bumper to bumper in that order. Waltrip and Labonte surged around Parsons entering the third turn. Labonte tried Waltrip on the inside down the stretch, but Darrell won by a car length. Parsons nipped Petty for third.

Parsons had passed Waltrip for the lead on the 185th lap of the 188-lapper, and according to Waltrip it was a move that suited both drivers.

"It's just a gamble, whatever you do," the Franklin, TN, star commented. "I just felt like with the number of cars involved, the thing to do was let Benny go and try to draft back by on the last lap. I'm not an advocate of sling-shotting, but it worked today.

"Benny was down in the middle of the speedway, and Terry and I were hooked in a draft. I knew if Terry didn't panic we could go to the front.

"I believe Benny thought his car was stronger than mine and Terry's and that he could buck the wind and hold us off. I think he anticipated a low pass, and we passed him on the outside.

"I knew when we came out of the fourth turn I would win the race."

Parsons was in front for 86 laps and Waltrip for 52 as the lead bounced among 13 drivers 51 times, but from lap 59 to lap 143 Darrell trailed.

"We jumped out there and led for awhile," the driver of the Junior Johnson Buick explained, "but it was a faster pace than we wanted to run and a faster pace than the car could run all day. It seemed like a good time just to watch the race, so I did. I paid to get in just like everybody else."

Parsons, an ex-PTA president who was known as stock car racing's Mr. Nice Guy, probably was the sentimental favorite of the crowd.

"If Benny had won that race I would have been tickled to death," one effervescent redhead said.

Stevie Waltrip, Darrell's wife, further commented, "I like that whole team, and everybody needs to win a race."

"But I'm glad we won, too."

When Waltrip pulled Terry Labonte with him on the pass, Parsons was stuck in third place.

"I wouldn't have minded Darrell getting in front of me if he just hadn't taken Terry with him," Parsons said. "I would have had a better shot at the checkered flag if I had been running second.

"I wanted to win this one so bad because I had such a good strong car. Besides, we need a win to get going."

Like a vase full of roses, it was gorgeous but it couldn't last forever, and Darrell Waltrip was the man who ended the Talladega 500 streak at 13 races, 13 faces. In the 14th Talladega 500, Waltrip beat Buddy Baker to become the first to win the summer classic twice. He also was the victor in 1979.

"This is the thrill of my racing career, to be the first repeat winner," the Franklin, TN, driver said. Then, with a grin, he told reporters, "I hope y'all make as big a deal out of this as you did out of the 13 different winners."

The streak began in 1969 with unsung Richard Brickhouse winning the track's first Winston Cup race. Then the Talladega 500's victory lane hosted Pete Hamilton, Bobby Allison, James Hylton, Dick Brooks, Richard Petty, Buddy Baker, Dave Marcis, Donnie Allison, Lennie Pond, Waltrip, Neil Bonnett and Ron Bouchard before Waltrip repeated.

Thirteen different winners in 13 races was the Winston Cup record. Perhaps records are made to be broken, but it is difficult to conceive of this one ever being surpassed.

Waltrip swept the second of the 1982 season's Winston Cup events at Talladega by holding off a final-lap slingshot attempt by Baker.

The last of 188 laps began with Waltrip, Baker, Terry Labonte, Cale Yarborough, Richard Petty and Bill Elliott locked in a bumper-to-bumper draft.

Waltrip and Baker put some daylight between themselves and the other four, then Waltrip beat Baker by less than a car length.

It was a close race, but it was evident all day that Waltrip had the field covered. Though there were 39 lead changes, he led 108 laps and put the muscle on Baker on the last circuit, thwarting Buddy's try at passing. Waltrip was in front for the final 17 laps.

"I never drove a car anywhere else that would run like that one and live for 500 miles," Darrell said of his Junior Johnson Buick.

"The car was so fast all day I could go to the front with ease. On the last pit stop I bogged the car down, but pretty soon I caught the leaders. I was surprised at how easily I caught them, and I knew then those guys were in trouble."

Waltrip said he didn't consider dropping back and try-

ing to draft by the leader on the last lap as he had drafted by Benny Parsons to win the Winston 500 in May.

"I was either going to be a hero or a you-know-what," he said. "If you put yourself in that position and get beat like Benny did in May..." He didn't finish the sentence. It wasn't one of Parsons' better moments.

"You feel like your whole career is riding on what you decide to do," Waltrip continued in the winner's press box interview. "If I had chosen to lead and finished fifth, there'd be more of y'all down there in the garage than up here."

Waltrip basked in the glow of his winning strategy: "I had everybody right where I wanted them—behind me."

Petty finished third, Yarborough fourth, Labonte fifth and Elliott sixth, with 10 cars on the lead lap at the end.

"I thought I could take Darrell on the last lap," said Baker. "I moved to the outside, and when I did the car broke traction and slipped a bit. I couldn't gather it back up in time. Still, I only lost the race by a few feet.

"Darn it," Baker added, "there wasn't any doubt in my mind. I felt I was in the right spot.

"Maybe he was a little stronger than I thought, though."

Petty said Baker waited too late to make his move and possibly carry Petty with him past Waltrip.

"I was in the position I wanted to be in," Richard said, "but Buddy never made a move, never pulled out. The man running in second place has to make the move first, but he just waited too late.

"It was a heck of a race, and I ran wide open most all day. For us to run this good at Talladega is like winning. That was the only thing missing—winning."

Yarborough said he thought the white flag, which signals the beginning of the final lap, was the checkered flag. "I just couldn't put it back together in time," he said.

Explained Labonte: "Cale got alongside me on the white flag lap, and I just got hung out there and lost the draft a little bit. There was nothing I could do once that happened."

Elliott said he attempted to follow Petty, decided Petty couldn't get through, then pulled behind Yarborough.

"All I could do was try to get by them at the finish line,

Darrell Waltrip wins the Talladega 500 to sweep the '82 events.

Waltrip (11) and Geoff Bodine (50) lead the field in the '82 Talladega 500.

but I couldn't."

Tim Richmond and Bobby Allison were in the lead draft six laps from the finish, but Allison had to pit, and Richmond's engine went sour. "We were going to run out of gas," said Allison, who finished 10th. "I was hoping for a caution flag."

On his previous pit stop—which should have been his last—Allison overshot his station and had to be pulled back, losing valuable time. Hoping to make it up, his crew didn't give him a full load of fuel.

"I dropped a valve," Richmond said. "I was just lucky I didn't have to pull it in. I was lucky it lasted until the end."

A crowd estimated at more than 90,000 saw Waltrip become the fourth Winston Cup driver to top $3 million in his career. He joined Petty, Yarborough and Allison in that corps, but Waltrip, who broke into the league in 1972, reached the figure sooner than the others did.

"The Frances built one whale of a race track here," Waltrip exulted after he exited his car—but he wasn't so pleased with the NASCAR points system.

It was Waltrip's seventh victory of the season. Terry

Labonte hadn't won a race. Yet Labonte was leading in the standings.

"There should be a bonus for winning the race," Waltrip said. "Racing is the name of the game, and the points system doesn't really favor a guy who races."

He wasn't saying Labonte didn't drive hard—just that the risk involved in trying to win sometimes resulted in a broken car and a drastic loss of points, and that when a charger did win he should receive an adequate portion of points.

Waltrip and Allison had won 12 of the 19 races in 1982, but the points read: Labonte, 2,812; Allison, 2,777; Waltrip, 2,691.

Waltrip had been far behind in points in 1981 before roaring to the throne, and he was getting hot again with two victories in the last three races. Had the charge begun?

"Yeah, I think so," Waltrip said. "It looks like we're getting a good handle on things. The points are starting to come our way."

Darrell Waltrip is one happy man after his Talladega victory.

1983

The fastest field that had ever started a Winston Cup event rolled off in what Dick Brooks predicted would be "the wildest, fastest, most competitive race anybody has ever seen anywhere."

It might not have been all of that, but no customer asked for his money back when it ended.

Six drivers, led by Cale Yarborough at a record 202.650, had navigated the speedway at better than 200 miles an hour in qualifying. The 40th and slowest qualifier did 192.808, a speed that would have won the pole six years before.

"The Winston 500 is going to be an incredible race," Bobby Allison predicted. "A lot of cars are running real well."

High speeds at Daytona and Talladega had generated much conversation, but Joe Ruttman said the home of the Winston 500 could handle the pace. "The track is big and wide, and it was designed for these speeds," he said.

Nobody doubted it would be a speed race, but Richard Petty stirred a spoonful of leavening into the conversation: "It's a 500-mile race, and the key to winning is to be around at the end. We're set up to be there."

And he was. As a star high school lineman, Petty never blocked better than he did on the last lap of the Winston 500. He held off Benny Parsons with a weaving ride along the frontstretch and won by half a car length before a crowd estimated at more than 110,000.

It was the Randleman, NC, immortal's first victory in the Winston 500. In an interview before the Winston 500 of the year before he had talked about that oversight and about his past and his future.

He was 44 at the time, and he was asked if retirement was in his sights.

"I'm going to be closer to 65 than to 40 when I quit," Petty declared, alluding to the traditional retirement age. He laughed and added, "It's going to be awhile before I quit."

Petty first heard retirement talk after the 1967 season when he won 27 races. "Everybody said, 'Well, you won all those races, and now you'll retire'," he recalled. "That was after Fred Lorenzen retired and said he had done all there was to do."

His immediate goal was scoring his 200th victory, Petty said. "Each one of my 195 wins over the years has been special to me and the team, and I think that when I win my 200th—well, that will be a special day for the Pettys.

"Back in 1979, when I started my 800th race, we all made a pretty big deal about that, but I think it will be an even bigger deal when I win No. 200.

"I've been lucky enough over the years to be able to race in a bunch of races, and it'll probably be a long time before any driver will top me in that department.

"I also think I've had my share of luck in being able to win as many races as I have over the years. The scheduling back in my early years of racing had a lot to do with my success.

"We would race from Hickory, NC, to Long Island, NY, and then maybe out west somewhere, all within the space of one week, and I was always fortunate enough to be driving some very good equipment."

In 1964, for instance, he competed in 61 events, including numerous short-track 100 milers. In those days several of the top teams passed up many such events.

"But then back in the '70s when the schedule was shortened it kind of changed the way a lot of racing teams operated," Petty said.

"Since then we've been running about 30 races a year, and the number of teams that are winning the races has increased quite a bit. It used to be that maybe two or three of us were winning a good part of the races, but now there are at least nine or 10 teams capable of winning every time the green flag is thrown.

"Darrell Waltrip was unusually lucky last year when he won 12 races. I don't think you'll see that happening much any more. Things are so competitive now that if you win one race you're doing fairly well. And if you win a couple of races you've had a good year."

And about the Winston 500 that he had never won?

"It's just another race," Petty answered with a shrug. "I'd like to win it, but if I don't I'm not going to get too excited about it.

"I don't know why I've never won the Winston 500. A lot of times you run well enough to win a race, but you just don't. The circumstances just aren't right. I liked the

73

Richard Petty in the winner's circle.

(above) The Skoal Patrol: Harry Gant (33), Phil (66) and Benny (55) Parsons.

Ontario track that closed, and I ran as well there as anywhere, but I never won a race there."

He said he wasn't superstitious. There was no Talladega jinx. "I believe in luck," Petty said, "but I don't believe you can do things to cause it or keep it away from you."

His only victory at the world's fastest speedway had been in the 1974 Talladega 500, and his average finish in 24 events at the track had been 14.5.

It wasn't exactly his favorite course. "I don't have a lot of fond memories of it," said Petty. "If I had started out winning and having good luck here I guess I would."

But his memories of the 1983 Winston 500 are fond ones, for in it he scored his 197th victory. His 200th and last win would come on July 4, 1984, in the Firecracker 400 at Daytona. He would retire after the 1992 season at age 55—as he said, closer to 65 than to 40.

Parsons couldn't solve Petty's shaky drive down the frontstretch on the last lap of the 1983 Winston 500.

Benny moaned: "When I went high, he went high; when I went low, he went low; when I went high, he went high. It was like he was reading my mind, like he was turning my steering wheel."

"Poor old Benny," the driver of the Petty Enterprises Pontiac remarked. "I had him inside and outside. He had to be concerned about Lake Speed and those other guys behind him, too. He had one eye on me and one behind him, and that kind of took away his concentration."

The final lap started with Petty, Parsons, Speed, Harry Gant, Terry Labonte and Bill Elliott in line for a wild finish.

Parsons tried Petty without success down the frontstretch. Speed tried to pass them both on the outside at the finish line, but he came up short and had to settle for third. Gant was fourth, Elliott fifth and Labonte sixth.

"Richard was strong, but if I could have gotten to him I could have beaten him," said Speed. "But we were geared to draft, and if I had tried to pull out earlier I would have been shuffled way back."

Phil Parsons was involved in one of the more memorable crashes in the track's history, a barrel-rolling episode that caused the remains of his car to be permanently exhibited in the International Motorsports Hall of Fame's museum next door.

And after Petty had survived 26 lead changes to finally win the Winston 500? "Oh, it means a lot," Richard said, "but ranking it with some other things I've done, it's not that important."

(above) Labonte receives service en route to a 6th place finish.
(below) The remains of Phil Parsons' car.

"It's going to rain at 3:28 today," Bud Moore announced. It was the morning of the Talladega 500, and the area hadn't seen rain since chariots were the preferred vehicles for racing. Moore drew blank stares at the speedway garage.

At 3:22, less than a minute after the cars crossed the finish line in the Talladega 500, the first wave of rain peppered the track. Moore wasn't perfect on his prediction, but at that moment he probably could have gotten a job as a TV weatherman.

It was that kind of day for Moore, the car owner, and Dale Earnhardt, the driver. Earnhardt led 42 laps in Moore's Ford, more than anyone else, and when he wasn't leading he was hounding whoever was. Moore and his men performed with dexterity and speed in the pits. And the last lap worked to perfection.

In fact, if the last lap had been a football play drawn on a blackboard, the coach would have been delighted with its execution.

A crowd estimated at 95,000 to 100,000 saw Earnhardt pass Darrell Waltrip on the backstretch, getting a boost in the draft from Bobby Allison who was two laps behind, when Allison fell in behind Earnhardt.

Then, when Waltrip attempted to pass Earnhardt on the frontstretch dogleg and Earnhardt needed to run up on the draft of a car or two, there were the lapped machines of Bobby Hillin and Kyle Petty, right where Dale wanted them. Waltrip's charge fell just short at the finish line.

"Those last three or four laps were pretty exciting," said Earnhardt. "During that time I was watching the slow cars and wondering when I'd catch them and wondering what Darrell was going to do.

"That was the most tense and excited I've been in the last few laps in a long time."

The Talladega 500's amazing streak had ended at 13 races, 13 faces the year before when Waltrip scored his second victory, but Earnhardt was the 14th man to visit victory lane in 15 events.

It was the first success at the world's biggest speedway for Earnhardt;—In 1993, he would win the Talladega 500 and thus tie Davey Allison as the track's winningest driver for the first quarter century, with eight victories in all types of races.

"Darrell tried to run me down into the infield, but I got

by, and I was ready to rub metal," Earnhardt said of his pass.

Later, the Mooresville, NC, driver said Waltrip did nothing wrong. "I had a couple more feet of track. He did the same thing I would have been doing, trying to close off the man behind. When he saw I was there he gave me room. He was just doing his best to win the race."

Waltrip was displeased with Allison's role in the scenario. Allison was two laps behind when he tagged onto Earnhardt's bumper and rode by Waltrip. On the frontstretch, Allison moved over and left the skirmish to Earnhardt and Waltrip. But his intervention may have been a key. It may have set up a draft that gave Earnhardt a spurt of speed.

"What's a car doing up there in the damn way?" Waltrip asked. "Is that fair?"

Darrell charged: "He ran me all the way to the wall. If Bobby had gotten out of the way, it would have been a little different. Bobby was in the way. He could have gotten out of the way. He knew what he was doing. That's the sign of a poor sport. It ain't the sign of nothing else."

Waltrip had led the previous 11 laps before Earnhardt passed him in the day's 45th lead change. "I never thought he'd get up there and away like that," Darrell said. "I figured I could pass him back. But I'm happy with second. I'm thankful for second."

Allison said he wasn't trying to hinder Waltrip. "I didn't have any further to go," he said. "I gave him plenty of room."

"I don't think I could have passed Darrell completely before the corner without Bobby," Earnhardt said. "But I think I could have passed him in the corner. Bobby stayed out of the way pretty good."

Later, Earnhardt commented, "I don't see where Bobby did anything wrong. He followed me. He was racing guys behind him to stay ahead of them."

Waltrip and Allison were fierce rivals. Darrell had edged Bobby in the battles for the national championship in 1981 and 1982, and Bobby would nip him in 1983.

For Earnhardt, catching the draft of the lapped cars of Petty and Hillin on the frontstretch was like finding

VICTORY
Talladeg

Earnhardt celebrates his first Talladega 500 victory.

The field for the '83 Talladega 500 takes the green flag.

Rudd and Bouchard battle for position.

Cale Yarborough leads the eventual winner, Dale Earnhardt.

money in the street.

"Darrell hadn't led much, and I just didn't know how strong he was," Earnhardt said. "But I saw Kyle and Hillin were going to be a factor over in the dogleg, and I felt my best shot at Darrell was on the backstretch. I thought that was where I'd better get by him.

"I knew he'd try to draft back by me, but I knew I'd pick up the draft from the slow cars, and it was just a matter of who would get to the line first.

"At the finish I looked over to see where Darrell was, and all I could see was Bobby Hillin's car."

Earnhardt had gone more than a year without a victory, but all of a sudden he had won two of the last three Winston Cup races.

"Things started turning around for us eight races ago," he said. "We've been doing some experimenting, and the car has been lasting longer."

General Motors cars won the first 15 races of the season, but since NASCAR changed engine rules the Fords had taken three of four events. "The Chevrolets were dominant today," Earnhardt said.

A four-car, last-lap shoot-out was a prospect until misfortune overtook Neil Bonnett and Ricky Rudd in the closing circuits.

Bonnett, driving relief for Tim Richmond, pitted on

the 176th round of the 188-lap race, but he had stretched his fuel too far, and the car stalled in the pit. The engine misfired, and the crew had to push-start the racer. They lost valuable seconds, and when Bonnett returned to the track he was some 400 yards behind the lead draft, running alone and unable to catch up. He finished third, with Richmond getting credit for the position.

Rudd was in the hunt, too, until his ignition went sour. His car limped the final 10 laps and, his chance to win turned into a 16th-place finish.

Earnhardt's average speed of 170.611 miles an hour made it the second-fastest Talladega 500 that had been run, but the race didn't begin with a hint it would be. The motor in Bonnett's car blew on the second lap, depositing oil and metal on the track, which triggered a mass wreck. The yellow flag waved for 12 laps while the crew hauled off cars and cleaned the racing surface, but

1984

WINSTON • 500
MAY 6, 1984

The speedway long ago had established itself as the most competitive racing venue in the world, but if any doubting Thomas anywhere could possibly have had reservations, they were dashed in the '84 Winston 500.

There were 75 lead changes, a record for any big-time event that still stands. The final swap came on the last lap when Cale Yarborough shot by Harry Gant and zoomed to victory.

The old record for a 500-mile auto race was 67 lead changes, set in the 1978 Talladega 500.

A crowd estimated at more than 115,000 saw Yarborough pass Gant entering the third turn of the last lap, then sweat out his own personal fuel crisis.

"It started running out of gas coming off the fourth turn on the last lap," said Yarborough, who scored his 80th Winston Cup victory. "I rocked the car back and forth with the steering wheel to pick up little pockets of gas. I barely had enough to cross the start-finish line."

Yarborough also ran out of gas before his final pit stop. "I coasted the last quarter of a lap that time," he said. "Then I had to run flat-out to catch back up."

Said Waddell Wilson, crew chief of the Ranier-Lundy Chevrolet team: "From our pit stop on the last caution flag we went 36 laps and ran out of gas. After that there were 35 laps left in the race, but Cale had to go so hard to run the leaders down that I was surprised he didn't run out before he did."

When Yarborough caught up with Gant, Benny Parsons and Buddy Baker after the first dry-tank incident, he contented himself with following until he made the race-winning move.

"Waddell told me on the radio to save fuel by not passing them," the Sardis, SC, driver said. "I drafted the rest of the way until the last lap."

How much gas did that save? "It saved enough for me to win the race," Yarborough answered. "That's exactly how much."

A four-car shoot-out was disrupted when Parsons and Baker pitted on the 177th lap for a quick drink of gasoline.

That left Yarborough and Gant. Cale took him on the inside lane entering the third turn and had enough power to beat Harry's inside try on the frontstretch.

The draft from lapped cars helped Yarborough, who said he doubted he could have won if he had not picked up the pull from Trevor Boys' racer on the frontstretch.

"When I came off turn two on the last lap, I looked the traffic situation over and laid it all out in my mind," Yarborough said. "I made the move when I did to pick up the draft to my advantage.

"Had I had a clean race track, I wouldn't have passed him on the backstretch. I'd have passed him on the front. But I knew he was going to play on those cars if I didn't."

The thrills weren't over when Yarborough beat Gant by a car length. Baker, Bobby Allison and Parsons crossed the line three abreast in the battle for third, finishing in that order.

For Gant, runner-up was a familiar slot. It was his 15th second-place finish in 168 Winston Cup races. He had won three.

A few years before, the press asked Gant about the "frustration" of finishing second so often. He replied: "I'd like to know I could finish second in every race. I'd be a rich man." He earned $31,780 in the Winston 500 and did not seem frustrated.

It was obvious Gant was a sitting duck (if one can call traveling 200 miles an hour sitting). Few in the crowd could have doubted Yarborough's powerful car would zip by Gant's racer.

"I tried to back off with five laps to go, but he wouldn't let me," said Gant, who wanted to be in position to try to slingshot Yarborough. "There wasn't anything I could do."

Gant glimpsed hope in the rearview mirror for a moment on the last lap—but just for a moment.

"Down in turn two I saw Cale fading back, and I thought I could get some more distance on him down the stretch," he said.

"Then here came Cale."

The pass was inevitable. "I tried to hold Cale off as long as I could," Gant said. "I gave him just enough room to get through."

Gant thought he could return the pass on the frontstretch, but the presence of Boys' car not only gave

1984 Winston 500 champion, Cale Yarborough.

Cale Yarborough claimed the pole position.

Yarborough a pull in the draft, it narrowed the playing field.

"I knew it was all over when I didn't have that outside route to take," Gant said. "If that car had not been there, I think I would have beaten him. I'm not blaming Boys by any means. Cale was just making the most of the race track.

"But I'm tickled to finish second. We ran a good race all day, and maybe next time it will be our turn."

Parsons said his car simply didn't get the mileage the winner's did. "We couldn't make it on the gas, and somehow Cale and Harry could," he commented. "I saw with about 150 miles to go that we wouldn't make it without an extra stop, so I decided to lead as many laps as I could.

What does that pay? A hundred dollars or so every other lap?

"Maybe some day I'll figure out how to run this race track properly. So far I haven't."

Said Baker: "The car ran really good all day, and it came down to the gas. We were probably the strongest out there. We took the lead from everyone at one point or another.

"We fought hard, and somehow we used more gas than the others. I'm really disappointed we didn't win, but I'm happy with the way the car ran."

Allison drove his sputtering car onto pit road on the next to last lap, thinking there were two laps to go after that one, but crew chief Gary Nelson waved him on. On

Yarborough passes Gant in the final lap on his way to victory.

the last lap he rocked the car to sling up enough gas to finish.

Dale Earnhardt and Darrell Waltrip had run 1-2 in the last race at the speedway, the 1983 Talladega 500, but they experienced only frustration in the '84 Winston 500.

Earnhardt sat in his car for 39 laps while his crew replaced a wheel assembly after a blown tire had caused his racer to hit the wall. "It's frustrating to wreck but equally frustrating to wait on a major repair during a race," he said. "I sometimes wonder if it's worth all the trouble to get back out there, but the points do add up during the course of a season. It's a necessary evil."

Waltrip was in street clothes, leaving the track with his wife Stevie and basset hound Frank when the race was barely a half-hour old. "I was worried about a lot of things," he said, "but I wasn't worried about blowing an engine. Now I guess I won't have to worry about anything."

Yarborough's speed of 172.988 miles an hour broke the Winston 500 record of 170.481 set in 1980.

Motorsports historians have called the 1984 Talladega 500 the greatest auto race ever run. Certainly no other speedway has ever hosted two such events as Talladega did in 1984.

Anyone who wondered what the track could do for an encore after the 75-lead-change Winston 500 got the answer in a 68-lead-change Talladega 500 that saw 10 cars involved in the ending, with three pictures from the photo finish camera required to determine the final order. Fifteen cars were in the lead lap at the climax.

Dale Earnhardt passed Terry Labonte on the last lap (that lead change eclipsed the Talladega 500 record of 67 set in 1978) and won by 1.66 seconds. Behind him in order were Buddy Baker, Labonte, Bobby Allison, Cale Yarborough, Darrell Waltrip, Harry Gant, Lake Speed, Tommy Ellis and Bill Elliott.

"This is the greatest race I've ever been involved in," Earnhardt said.

Jubilant track officials called it "the most competitive race in NASCAR history."

Earnhardt made his move on Labonte as they approached the third turn. Baker hooked up with Earnhardt, and they shot around the leader. Then Terry and Buddy got to racing side by side on the frontstretch, a maneuver which damaged the draft and allowed Earnhardt to win by the length of a football field and a half.

"Most exciting one I've ever driven in," Earnhardt exclaimed.

The Mooresville, NC, driver continued: "In a race like that, you know where you want to be, and my car worked good enough that I was where I wanted to be.

"Terry slowed the pace a little down the backstretch to cool the tires down. When he went low going into the third turn, I went outside and Buddy went with me.

"The biggest thing I was worried about was Buddy. I knew he would try to slingshot me in the trioval. But thankfully he and Terry got a little messed up back there, and I pulled away coming off the fourth turn."

Labonte didn't want the lead going into the final lap. He didn't care to be a sitting duck for a slingshot maneuver, but he couldn't figure out a way to give it up. If he had pulled out and lost the draft he might have ended up 10th.

"I wanted to be in second place going into the last lap," he said, "but I couldn't find a way to get there without going way back. So all I could do was hope they got side by side behind me.

"Going into the last lap, I saw Buddy and Dale side by side, and I really thought things looked great.

"But then Dale came flying past me, and that was it. He just ran me down. He was too strong. I figured that out before he got me on the last lap.

"There were so many cars out there with a chance to win that you really didn't know what to do."

Said Baker: "I never ran so hard for so long in my life."

Buddy spent more time on the point than any of the other 15 leaders. He led 41 laps and Earnhardt 40.

Baker had mixed emotions after the photo finish camera ruled him runner-up.

"First of all, you couldn't have asked for a more perfect day," he said. "Can you believe a day this cool at the end of July in Alabama?

"I ran a hard race, but unfortunately for me everybody else was there at the end, too.

"I sort of got caught out of position and couldn't make the move that I wanted to make. I'll bet it was a heck of a show for the people in the stands at the finish."

At first, Labonte was posted in the No. 2 spot, but that changed when the photos were developed. "I thought I had second spot over Labonte because his door post was behind mine as we went across the line," Baker said. "I was worried because it took so long to decide. I kept thinking that those Chevrolet nose pieces must be longer than I thought."

There had been rumbling about the 200-mph speeds, some saying NASCAR should do something to cut the pace.

"I guess we squashed the theory—with all the drivers going for the win there at the end—about 200 being unsafe," Baker said. "It's just like I've said before, it all depends on who's going 200 and where they are racing. I felt perfectly secure with the speed and the drivers around me. This track can handle 200, maybe even a little more."

Allison did all he could do, he said. "I wasn't where I wanted to be at the end, but I was as close to the front as

Earnhardt returns to victory land in the '84 Talladega 500.

Ron Bouchard runs past Buddy Baker in the '84 Talladega.

Geoff Bodine (5) and Kyle Petty (7) mix it up.

Earnhardt's crew springs into action.

the car would allow me to be.

"I just had to hang on out there. I wanted to go to the front, but I couldn't get there. There just wasn't anything that I could do. There was no strategy out there, with so many cars and all of us trying to get up in the pack.

"It must have been one heck of a show. I tried my best, but so did everyone else."

The deadly potential of such a finish remained just that, potential. "It was like basketball," Allison said. "Don't foul anyone and hope no one fouls you."

An estimated 94,000 fans saw Earnhardt drive the RCR Enterprises Chevrolet to his first Winston Cup victory since he won the 1983 Talladega 500.

NASCAR must have breathed a sigh of relief, for it no longer faced the prospect of Earnhardt winning the championship without winning a race. Thanks largely to four runner-up finishes, Dale was atop the 1984 standings. (He didn't win the title anyway. Labonte did, while Earnhardt finished fourth.)

"I really wasn't worried about whether I'd ever win another race," Earnhardt said. "I was just wondering which one it was going to be. This is my first win since teaming up with Richard Childress, and it's one I cherish. But I cherish them all. I won here last year in Bud Moore's Ford, and I'll always remember that one.

"Talladega is the fastest and most competitive track.

Eight of us had a chance there at the end, and there was no telling who would win. Everybody in that lead bunch did a great job of driving. When one car would start vibrating, everybody would back off."

There was one spectacular crash. On the 156th lap, Trevor Boys' car hit an oil spill coming into the frontstretch dogleg, skidded 100 yards upside down and did a couple of flips across the grass in front of pit road. He walked away.

"It was just one of those things that happen in racing," said Boys. "The car was running great, and I was in the lead pack. I made the decision that if everything was working so good and if I needed some experience, why not get it from leading the race?

"I pulled out to make my move to the front, but Tommy Ellis tagged me on the right rear quarter panel as I went by. The next thing I knew, I just took off. All I could see at the start of the wreck was dirt, dust and weeds, so I closed my eyes because I figured I didn't really want to see any more."

Bill Elliott not only captured races and purses in 1985, he captured the imagination of the public. Elliott was that most enduring figure of American folklore, the wily country boy who outfoxed and outdid the big mules.

At least in the minds of the fans.

Elliott probably was called Huckleberry Finn more than Huckleberry Finn was. A redhead with a flat Georgia drawl, he was the driver for a team located not in the Charlotte area-the hub of stock car racing-but in Dawsonville, GA, a hamlet of 347 souls.

His brother Ernie, who was 37, built bulletproof engines (no doubt under a shade tree) and Bill, who was 29, drove them to victory (no doubt after milking the cows and slopping the pigs that morning).

In 1985, Bill Elliott won 11 Winston Cup races, all on superspeedways, and earned $2,383,186. His fans sniffed that the fact Darrell Waltrip rather than Elliott won the national championship said more about the title format than about their hero. He would have beaten Waltrip under the methods used by CART, Formula One, IMSA GT and the world endurance series.

Some said no one would ever earn the Winston Million, but Elliott grabbed it the first year it was available. R.J. Reynolds posted a million-dollar bonus to any driver who could win three of the Big Four—the Daytona 500, the Winston 500, Charlotte's World 600 and Darlington's Southern 500. Only the World 600 escaped Elliott.

The frustration the other teams felt was voiced simply but eloquently by Neil Bonnett during a recess at Talladega. "If I knew what they've got I'd be out there putting it on my car instead of sitting here eating this sandwich."

Actually, Elliott's Ford team, Melling Racing, was a big, slick outfit, not a team sharing a stable with plowhorses. Plowing horsepower into its engines was its specialty.

Elliott won at Daytona, Atlanta and Darlington, then stunned Talladega by winning the Winston 500 pole with a NASCAR record run of 209.398 miles an hour, much faster than Cale Yarborough's 205.679.

Richard Petty was prompted to say that he had seen teams as dominant as Elliott's, but that they didn't adver-tise their superiority as Elliott's had. One was his own.

"I've had it from time to time," he said of the big edge. "David Pearson has. Junior Johnson's cars have. But everybody played it close to the vest. They were afraid to show they had it because they were afraid NASCAR would jack around the rules. They did just what they had to do to put on a race."

NASCAR indeed made a rules change before the Winston 500, raising the Fords a half inch and lowering the GM products a half inch. It might have slowed Elliott some, but it was far from an equalizer.

"I think every time you get a serious challenge from someone or a rule change, there's that much more drive to come back and have a good run," Ernie Elliott said after time trials. "That's what makes a good team."

Awesome Bill from Dawsonville performed what is perhaps the most memorable come-back in racing history in the Winston 500. Under green, he zoomed from five miles behind to win.

The fastest stock car driver won at the fastest speedway in appropriate fashion. His average speed of 186.288 miles an hour made it the fastest 500-mile automobile race anyone had ever run. The previous record was 177.602 in the 1980 Daytona 500 that Buddy Baker won. Only two caution flags waved in the Winston 500, each for four laps. The race went 159 laps without a caution.

A crowd estimated at 122,000 thought Elliott's day was over when it had barely dawned. Smoke poured out from under the hood on the 48th lap, and he drove to his pit, apparently the victim of an engine failure. But that wasn't the case.

"The oil line came loose at the oil pump, I think," Elliott said. "It felt like I sat there six or 10 laps instead of a lap and a half. But they raised the hood and got it fixed faster than I thought they would."

Did he panic? "Yeah, really, I did."

Did he believe he could make up the deficit?

"Honestly, no."

When Elliott returned to the track after a pit stop of a minute and nine seconds, he was just 200 yards shy of

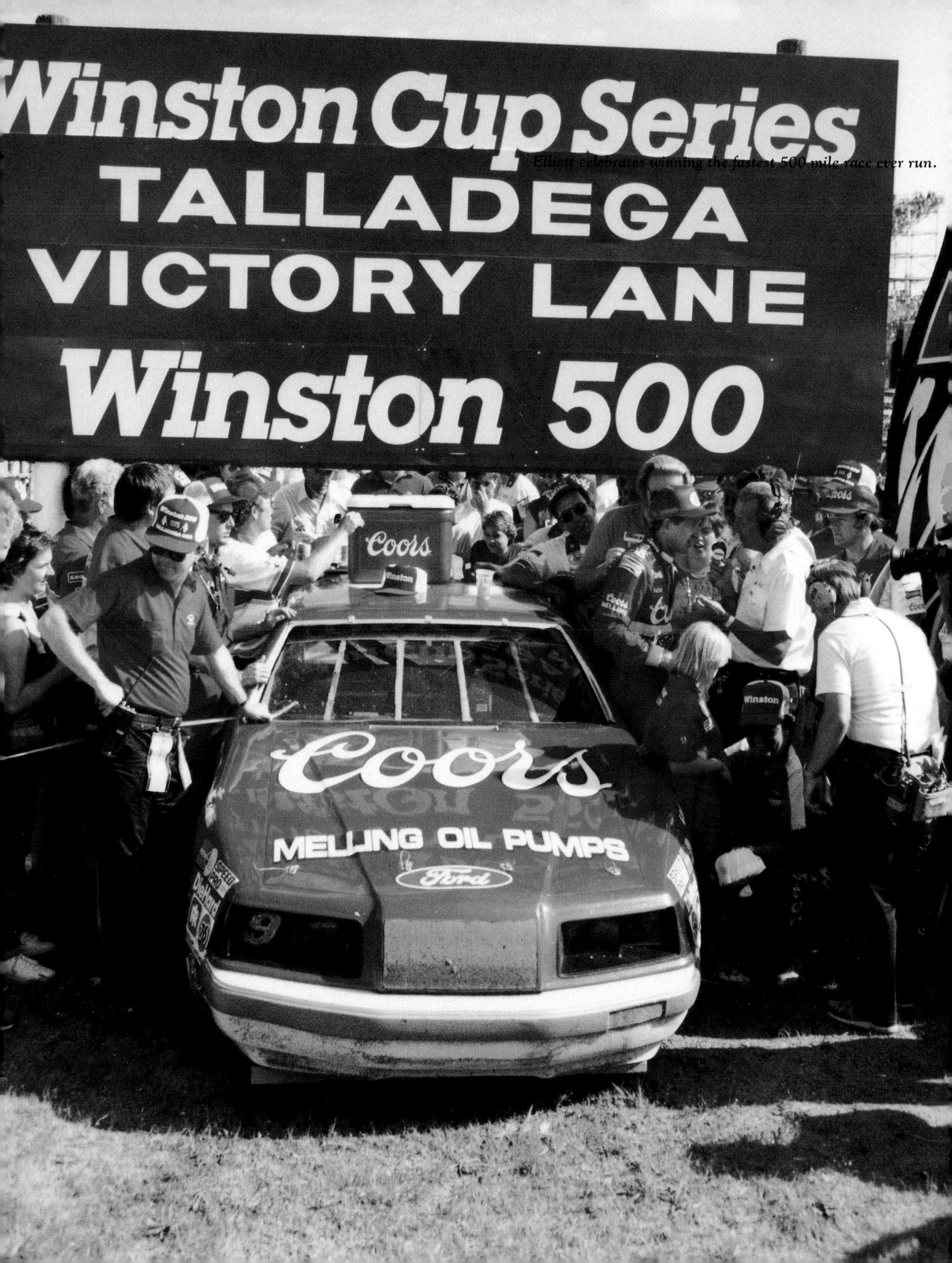

Winston Cup Series
TALLADEGA
VICTORY LANE
Winston 500

Elliott celebrates winning the fastest 500 mile race ever run.

Coors

Coors

Coors

MELLING OIL PUMPS

Ford

9

(above) Two NASCAR greats, Bobby Allison and Cale Yarborough battle in turn four.
(left) Junior Johnson's Bud machines lead the field.

Miss Talladega, Allison Norton, helps Elliott celebrate his win.

being two laps down.

Now pitting several laps out of sync with the leaders, Elliott would gain on their stops and lose on his own. On the track he was turning some laps a second faster than the competition.

On the 145th lap Elliott finally passed Cale Yarborough for first place. He stayed there until everyone pitted under the first caution flag.

Yarborough was out front on the restart, but Elliott reclaimed the lead a few laps later with the day's 27th lead change and never lost it. He was turning laps at 205 miles an hour as he pulled away at the finish. He won by 1.72 seconds.

The last lap wasn't totally without drama, however. Yarborough was running second and Kyle Petty was third as it began. Petty passed him on the outside entering the third turn, and they finished side by side, with Petty notching the runner-up slot to equal his best Winston Cup finish. Bobby Allison slingshotted around Ricky Rudd to finish fourth, a lap down.

Elliott had now won four of the first five superspeedway races of the season. That hadn't happened since 1976 when David Pearson did it. Elliott reached the $2 million figure in earnings in the Winston 500. He leaped from $1

million to $2 million in just 38 races, a Winston Cup record.

His performance in the Winston 500 was virtuoso stuff. "Getting behind like that is tough on everything, the driver, the car, the crew," Elliott said. "When you're in the lead draft you can relax a little, but when you're behind you have to drive as fast as you can."

Elliott admitted his success and sudden celebrity were taking an emotional toll. "Sure, I'm more or less the organizer at the shop. I have to do personal appearances. Then I have to get up on Sunday morning and hope everything is all right."

How did it feel to reach star status? "I don't consider myself that," he said. "I go out and don't act different from anybody else, but everybody looks at you and tries to put you on a pedestal. Sometimes it is hard."

Kyle Petty said he felt as if he won the race because he outdueled Yarborough. "It used to be that if you were going to win at Talladega you had to outrun the No. 28 car," he said. "I did, so I feel like I won.

"When we were side by side I said a quick prayer and poured on the coal. The Lord must have heard me first because I know Cale was probably talking to him, too."

Bill Elliott was the story of the 1985 Winston Cup season as he won a record 11 superspeedway races and the Winston Million, but if his fans had joked that their man could whip the field on seven cylinders, they learned at Talladega that wasn't true.

Elliott, bidding for his ninth Winston Cup victory of the season, had led 100 laps and was in front when the green flag waved on the 167th circuit of the 188-lap Talladega 500 to end a caution period.

Cale Yarborough's car shot into the lead, while Elliott's dropped steadily back. He had lost a cylinder to a malady his shocked mechanics couldn't identify.

Yarborough's Ford, Neil Bonnett's Chevrolet and Ron Bouchard's Buick were running bumper to bumper until the start of the final lap. Bouchard tried to overtake Bonnett at the starting line before they even reached the first turn, and they got to racing between themselves. Yarborough picked up the draft of a couple of lapped cars, and was gone. He won by a second over Bonnett. Bouchard was third and Elliott fourth.

Could Yarborough have whipped Elliott if Elliott's engine hadn't soured?

"We'll never know, will we?" Yarborough answered.

"We thought we could have beaten Cale at the end if it came down to the two of us," Elliott said, "but we'll have to wait 'til another time to see."

Yarborough said it gladdened his heart to see Bouchard pull out of line and damage the draft during the showdown, "but what tickled me most was to see those two lapped cars in front of me so I could draft off them.

"But I was awful pleased when I saw Bouchard and Bonnett running side by side. I knew it was over then."

"I was trying to get in the right position there at the end," Bouchard said. "Neil wasn't real strong, and I wanted to get in between them, but he wouldn't let me.

"When I got up next to him, he ran into the grass on the backstretch and bent the front end of my car up.

"I was stronger than Neil, and I tried to get by him. It was either give him a shot to win or me, and I wanted the shot myself." Bouchard's crippled racer dropped off the pace after they tangled, and Bonnett had second secured.

Said Bonnett: "Ron and I got to racing, and we let Cale drive away. I didn't think Ron would do that, but when he did I knew neither one of us would win."

Bonnett had planned to challenge Yarborough on the backstretch, but it didn't work out. "I thought sure Bouchard would wait 'til the backstretch to make his move," Bonnett said. "We might not have overtaken Cale, but we could have given him a run for it."

Bouchard said his strategy was logical. "I was going for the win. I knew I couldn't overtake the leader until I got by Neil first. So I made my move early to try to get by Neil."

It was Bonnett's second-straight runner-up performance. He was second to Elliott at Pocono the week before.

Elliott led Bouchard and Bonnett by half a lap when Geoff Bodine hit the wall to produce the final caution period of the 17th Talladega 500. Yarborough was nearly a lap behind, but the yellow flag enabled him to catch up.

The Sardis, SC, veteran made up the lap in his Ranier-Lundy Ford to win. Yarborough dropped a circuit near the middle of the race when he pitted before the caution car picked up the leaders during a yellow period.

"The car handled super good all day," Yarborough said. "That was the main factor in my being there at the end. My car was working better than Bill's."

The crowd of 95,000 was stunned to see Elliott's racer fall back on the restart.

And how did he react when he saw Elliott's racer drop off the pace?

"Hallelujah"

It was Yarborough's first victory since he won at Pocono on June 10, 1984.

"With the team I've got, I didn't see any way we could get skunked, go a whole year and not win one," he said. "Of course, I can say that now that I've won one. But I mean it."

The start of the race was delayed by a downpour that, one writer said, "would have sent Noah reaching for his hammer and nails." It left spectators' cars stuck in the parking lot. It affected at least one race car, too. Kyle Petty's delay in the garage area after a wreck was extend-

DAVEY ALLISON

Elliott and Earnhardt lead the way.

ed by the goo his racer collected when it slid into the infield.

"We must have pulled at least a hundred pounds of mud out of the car in the garage," he said. "We had to take one header pipe off because it was so full of mud, and we had to dig about a foot of mud out of the other one." He returned to the race after his mechanics hosed off his car.

Talladega races frequently are good for unusual happenings, and this one was no different.

Driver Dale Earnhardt suffered superficial facial cuts when a UFO flew through his windshield, spraying him with a shower of glass. When he pitted, a crewman removed a three-foot length of another car's driveshaft from his cockpit. It arrived with such force that it bent the rollbar—but fortunately for Dale, it didn't bend him.

A windshield support was broken, but Earnhardt's crew replaced the windshieldanyway, securing the new one with yards of duct tape. Earnhardt drove on, peering around the tape, finally holding his collapsing windshield in place with one hand.

"A driveshaft came out of somebody's car in the third turn," Yarborough said. "I drove over it and saw it go through Earnhardt's windshield. I knew if it hit him he was going to be in trouble."

Someone may have thrown something on the track and caused Phil Parsons to crash.

"I saw something come out of the stands," Parsons said after his car hit the wall near the midpoint of the race. "As soon as it hit the track my tire blew."

The youngster was driving the race of his life. He had been running in the lead five-car draft.

"I'm terribly disappointed," he said. "We had a car that was capable of winning the race. I went for the lead once over on the backstretch, and I got it.

"We just wanted to hang on to the lead draft, and we were riding along doing that."

A future star, Davey Allison of nearby Hueytown, made his Winston Cup debut and ran 10th, two laps behind Yarborough.

"There's a heck of a lot of difference in running 500 miles as compared to 300 miles," the former ARCA standout said as he massaged his neck after the race. "The longest race I had ever run before today was 312 miles. I'm glad to get the first one out of the way."

Cale Yarborough is pleased with his '85 Talladega win.

It was the year of the "Over-the-Hill Gang" in sports. First, 46-year-old Jack Nicklaus won the Masters. Then 54-year-old Bill Shoemaker won the Kentucky Derby.

Then 48-year-old Bobby Allison won the Winston 500 and became the oldest victor in the history of Winston Cup racing.

Allison started racing when he was a teenager, and he used the alias "Bob Sunderman" to hide his identity from his parents. But an estimated 130,000 witnesses knew who was in that Buick when it crossed the finish stripe, and they knew any fears that Bobby Allison might be washed up were groundless.

In 1985, Allison had quit the morale-ravaged DiGard team and driven for himself without success. He had joined the Stavola Brothers team in 1986, but that young outfit hadn't won.

Allison had gone 55 races without a triumph. He hadn't been to a victory lane since he took the 1964 World 600 at Charlotte.

But the move he put on Dale Earnhardt, one of the toughest foes in racing, in the fourth turn of the last lap of the Winston 500 was all guts and verve and experience. Earnhardt nosed ahead of him on the inside of turn No. 3, but Allison re-passed him on the outside in No. 4.

Ned Jarrett, the ex-driver turned broadcaster, suggested to Bobby during the victory lane ceremony that some folks had thought he was over the hill. "Ned, neither one of us are," he answered, "and we don't care what they think."

Allison replaced Richard Petty as the oldest Winston Cup winner. Petty was 47 when he took the 1984 Firecracker 400 at Daytona.

The press asked Allison if, during the long drought, he wondered if he might never win again.

"I've wondered all through my career if I was ever going to win again," the Hueytown, AL, star parried. "When I was 21 years old I won 19 short track races in a row and lost the 20th and wondered if I'd ever win again."

It was an immensely popular victory, and Allison could be forgiven a little exaggeration. "We've been trying to break a losing streak for awhile," he said, "and I can't

think of a better place than here at home. There were about 175,000 screaming Alabamans out there."

It was a fun post-race press conference.

A young reporter asked him if winning was as thrilling as ever. "You'll never understand until you get 48 years old and try to get out of bed," Allison answered.

How did he feel about being the oldest man to win a Winston Cup race? "It feels real good, and you can tell those other two youngsters who just won to hang in there," he answered, referring to Nicklaus and Shoemaker.

Bill Elliott was zooming toward his second straight Winston 500 victory when his engine blew, 14 laps from the finish, leaving the trophy to Allison. Elliott had dominated the race, only to drop the candy in the closing minutes. He had led 118 laps of the 188-lap event.

"I'm a little disappointed, but I'm not mad, I'm not sad, and I'm not glad," Elliott said. "I'm not feeling much of anything right now."

Elliott won the pole with a world-record qualifying run of 212.229 miles an hour, topping the 209.274 of No. 2 qualifier Allison by nearly three miles. Forty-one of the 42 starters qualified at better than 200 miles an hour, and since the last two were in on provisional starts rather than speed, it was technically called the first all-200 field in stock car history.

In fact, everything had gone so well for Elliott that he was uneasy. "It's been such a great week that I prepared myself every lap for something to go wrong," the Ford driver said. "Everything was going too good the whole day until the motor finally blew up. I just had a funny feeling all day something would happen."

Allison had demonstrated throughout the afternoon that he had the second-strongest car, but it wasn't in the same class as Elliott's. Elliott had about an eight-length lead when a piston broke.

"We had reserve on everybody else all day, but Bill had us beaten," Allison confirmed.

Still, Allison probably could take some of the credit for Elliott's car not finishing. He chased him persistently.

"I think that certainly did contribute to it," Bobby said. "I always felt that if a guy didn't have to work his equip-

Bobby Allison wears the top hat after his '86 Winston 500 victory.

Rusty Wallace drafts with Buddy Baker.

Jimmy Means (52) races with Phil Parsons (66).

Bobby Allison wins his third Winston 500 in 1986.

ment, the chances of it failing were slim. But we ran him hard, and something failed."

Elliott's departure didn't gift-wrap the victory for Allison, however. He still had to out-duel Earnhardt.

Elliott's blown engine produced a caution period, and the race resumed under green on lap 179. Allison sped from third place to first on 183.

The final lap began with Allison, Earnhardt and Buddy Baker bumper to bumper. Earnhardt took the inside route and nosed ahead of Allison in the third corner, but Allison surprisingly took him on the outside in four and won by two car lengths.

Allison said he felt confident he could beat Earnhardt. "Our car handled real good up high," he explained. "I knew when we went up into the gray that the car stuck a little better, so I knew on the last lap I had that cushion."

He said he took one lane and gave Earnhardt three in case Earnhardt's car slid. "He got up there, but he got bad out of shape," Allison explained. "I stayed in shape and out-accelerated him."

Said Earnhardt: "I took a shot at the end of the straightaway and got by him, but he was awfully strong and got right back by me. He was just too strong on that short deal.

"I feel if I could have come all the way by him going into a corner it might have made a difference. If Baker and I had tucked tight in a draft it might have made a difference."

Earnhardt's car was erratic, though. "When Dale got sideways, I didn't have the horsepower to make a move," Baker said.

Allison wasn't near any of the day's wrecks, but something did fly through his windshield. He was fortunate that it happened during a caution period, and his crew had time to change the windshield without losing much ground.

"I didn't see anything," Allison said. "But wham! All of a sudden my windshield was destroyed, and my mouth was full of glass. It had to have been a rock or something about the size of a baseball."

Though it was contested by the fastest field in stock car history, the race was run at an average speed of just 157.698, since the caution flag waved for 42 laps.

Bobby Hillin pulled onto pit road after he'd won the Talladega 500, and he drove all the way to the end of the boulevard, looking like a bewildered kitten nobody wanted.

He stopped, shifted his Buick into reverse and began backtracking. Finally, somebody hailed him and shooed him and his car into victory lane, which is about midway along pit road.

"I kept looking," Hillin explained later. "I've seen people win races, and everybody leads them in. But nobody led me in. I got there and the gate was closed. I thought maybe I didn't win."

His crewmen could be excused; they weren't experienced at herding their driver into the magic circle. In fact, they probably were turning cartwheels out in the infield when he won because he had never been first in a Winston Cup race before.

Hillin's victory was the second and final installment on a Talladega dream season for Stavola Bros. Racing.

Bobby Allison, 48, won the Winston 500 and became the oldest man ever to win a Winston Cup race.

Bobby Hillin, 22, won the Talladega 500 and became the youngest man ever to win a Winston Cup race on a superspeedway.

At first it was announced in the press box that Hillin was the youngest ever to win any WC event, but a more thorough check revealed he was third-youngest.

His victory didn't quite measure up to the great Talladega 500 upsets, such as James Hylton's in 1972, Dick Brooks' in 1973 and Ron Bouchard's in 1981, but it was a delightful surprise.

Hillin had threatened at the giant sister tracks that year. He had been fourth in the Daytona 500, fourth in the Winston 500 and third in Daytona's Firecracker 400. He was a win looking for a place to happen.

It was one of the greatest automobile races ever run. Twenty-six of the 40 drivers led the race to destroy a Winston Cup record. The previous high was 17 leaders in the 1975 Talladega 500 and in the 1982 Southern 500 at Darlington.

There were 48 lead changes, the last occurring when Hillin passed Tim Richmond on the 180th lap of the 188-lap event.

The final circuit began with Hillin leading a swarm of 11 other cars. He and Richmond and Rusty Wallace zoomed away as a crash in the first and second turns eliminated Allison, Rick Wilson and Jim Sauter and slowed the others.

Hillin drove a weaving path on the frontstretch dogleg, and neither Richmond nor Wallace could slingshot by him at the finish. He beat Richmond by half a car length, and Wallace finished beside Richmond.

"My car was handling so good I didn't take my foot off the floor," Hillin said, describing the last lap. "The gas pedal was burning a hole in my foot.

"I pulled way out and way over to keep Ricky from getting in my draft," continued Hillin (who didn't know Wallace was driving relief for Ricky Rudd). "I didn't do it slowly. I did it drastically.

"If he had got beside me I was prepared to do some short-track banging if I'd had to.

"I guess Ricky and Richmond were fighting among themselves the last 100 yards, and that helped me."

Hillin faced a question nearly as old as the speedway itself. Should he lead at the beginning of the final lap or be second and try to slingshot?

"When I got up to Bobby Allison and Tim Richmond, I asked myself whether I needed to pass or wait," the Midland, TX, driver said. "But I'd been passing them all week in practice and decided to go on with it."

Richmond was the hottest driver in stock car racing. He had won three of the four most recent races (and would win the one after Talladega, at Watkins Glen), but before the Talladega 500 he was pessimistic about his car's chances.

He called his runner-up finish "just like a win for us. The wreck on the second turn on the last lap made me lose the draft, and I lost my shot at a win."

Wallace, a Pontiac driver, wasn't unhappy about running third in a Ford he'd never been in before.

"I'm tickled to be able to help a team like Bud Moore's and give Ricky credit," he said. "Before today I had no idea what another car felt like. I don't know how the other Thunderbirds are, but this car stuck right to the

Ahead of the pack at the '86 Talladega 500.

Cale Yarborough tries for the inside position.

race track like it was supposed to."

Wallace's engine blew early in the day, and he subbed for Rudd, who was recovering from the flu.

It was a crash-marred race. A crowd estimated at 105,000 saw the caution flag wave nine times for 45 laps.

A key crackup occurred on lap 160. It eliminated contenders Harry Gant, Geoff Bodine, Cale Yarborough and Buddy Baker and almost benched Hillin.

"Phil Parsons and Harry Gant were bumping in turn two like they were on a short track," Hillin said. "They were still bumping on the backstretch, and Harry got up against the wall, and I was there. He had slid sideways,

and my front bumper hit his rear bumper."

The last-lap crash was a doozy. Kyle Petty, who got tagged but drove on to the finish, had a colorful comment: "It really seemed like everybody got a little bit crazy on the last lap, and I don't know if it was because of the heat, the competition, a full moon or what."

Neil Bonnett, who was injured in a crash at Pocono the week before, turned his Junior Johnson Chevy over to young Davey Allison, his Hueytown neighbor, who had won four ARCA races at Talladega but who didn't have a regular Winston Cup ride. Davey finished seventh after running with the leaders all day and leading a couple of

Bobby Hillin is excited about his '86 Talladega 500 win.

times himself. One newspaper account said he "proved he could duel with the best at speeds over 200 miles an hour."

"He ran a good strong race, stayed out of trouble and brought the car home in one piece and in the lead pack," said Johnson. "His stock as to getting a regular ride definitely went up with a lot of people today."

Hillin's stock went up, too. The youngster more than held his own in a fierce race contested on a brutally hot afternoon. He wasn't wearing a dry thread when it was over, but he appeared relatively fresh.

"I was going good until the last 30 laps, and I ran out of sweat," Hillin said. "I didn't have any sweat left. But when I was leading that sucker I didn't know it was hot."

Davey Allison cracked a joke to a caller on Monday after the Winston 500. "I'm having to bend over real far to pick up the phone," he said at his Hueytown, AL, home.

Okay, why?

"Because I'm walking on Cloud Nine."

He should have been. At 26, he had just won his first Winston Cup race, appropriately before the home folks at Talladega. He had become the first rookie to win a big league stock car event since Ron Bouchard did it in the 1981 Talladega 500, and he was on his way to Rookie of the Year honors.

What does a young man do in the evening hours when he has earned $71,250?

"We had a little celebration at Dad's house," he said. "He invited us over, and we were there 'til about 1 this morning."

At 1:30 Sunday afternoon no one would have guessed that Bobby Allison, Davey's father and Hueytown neighbor, would have been partying that night.

A tire blew, and his car became airborne, wiping out a 35-yard section of catch fence in front of the frontstretch grandstand. The fence threw the car back onto the racing surface, and the racer was destroyed.

"I've got a couple of bruises," Bobby said Monday, "but, considering, I'm in perfect shape. Something stuck a hole in my right hand, and the meat is sore. People say, 'I'm glad you're not hurt,' and then they grab it and squeeze it hard."

Davey dominated the race in his Ranier-Lundy Ford. He would pull away from the competition, a caution flag would bunch the field, and then he would do it again. That became a familiar sight. He led 101 of the 178 laps and beat Terry Labonte by less than a second. Kyle Petty was third, Dale Earnhardt fourth and Bobby Hillin fifth.

The race was stopped 10 laps short of regulation because of approaching darkness after all the teams were told well in advance.

"To get my first Winston Cup win at Talladega is fantastic," Davey said. "I saw the fans standing in the grandstand, waving me on. I couldn't hear them cheering, but I knew they were cheering for us, and it gave me cold chills. I always wanted to win my first one here, but if I'd won one before we got here it wouldn't have broken my heart. I'd like to start a family tradition. I'd like to come back and win it again."

A year before, Bobby Allison had taken the Winston 500, becoming, at 48, the oldest man ever to win a Winston Cup race.

Davey's victory was his fifth at Talladega, and that made him the track's winningest driver. The other four came in ARCA races. He was competing in just his 14th Winston Cup event.

"This car was so strong all day that I could do anything I wanted to," he said. "It handled so well that it ran right on the bottom of the track. It's something to be able to do whatever you want to with a car on a track like this one."

Earnhardt had won four straight Winston Cup events. "Davey ran a heck of a race," he said. "He stayed out front by himself all day. My car ran good, but we were lucky to finish in the top five."

Labonte said he was pleased to finish second. "My car ran super all day. It handled super. It's just hard to outrun a Thunderbird. They have so much more aerodynamics and run so much faster down the straightaways. We could catch them in the corners, but we just couldn't outrun them on the straightaways."

Kyle Petty said he might have finished second if the race hadn't been shortened. "Davey would have been hard to run down, but it wouldn't have hurt to finish all 188 laps. We laid the spoiler down the last 50 laps, and the car was really stout the rest of the way."

Bill Elliott won the pole at 212.809 miles an hour, and when the curtain fell on the first quarter-century of racing at Talladega, that was the record for the Winston Cup circuit. A crowd estimated at 135,000 saw the fastest field in stock car history take the flag. It averaged 207.049. But this wasn't to be Elliott's day. He was running second when his car began slowing on the 101st lap. Davey lapped him on 148, and his machine finally quit on 150.

"The Thunderbird worked pretty good, ran pretty good, but it didn't want to live until the end of the day,"

Uncool Racestoppers help Davey Allison celebrate his first big league win

Davey Allison's pit crew kept him out front all day in the '87 Winston 500.

Elliott said. "Evidently it dropped a valve or something."

It was a week of ups and downs for the Allison family. On Thursday, Bobby and Davey captured two of the first three starting positions for the Winston 500. On Friday, Bobby's son Clifford won a 50-lap Late Model feature in Birmingham. On Saturday, Bobby fell out of an All Pro race in Birmingham early. On Sunday, Bobby's car hit the catch fence, and Davey's went to victory lane.

A tire blew on Bobby's car on the 22nd lap, and the 3,500-pound machine got airborne. It tagged the fence and fell back onto the track, triggering a wreck that eliminated the racers of Cale Yarborough and Ron Bouchard. Also caught in it were those of Darrell Waltrip, Mike Waltrip, Alan Kulwicki, Richard Petty and Benny Parsons.

"The right rear tire went down," Bobby said. "I think I ran over something. I felt something bouncing around under the car going through the trioval, then I got up in the air and around backwards, and when I did, there was nothing I could do at all then. The car was really running good, too.."

Said Davey: "My heart sank. That was the most scared I've ever been in my life. I looked up in the mirror and saw Dad against the fence, and that probably was the lowest emotionally I've ever been.

"I came back by and saw him getting out of the car, and that lifted my heart back where it should be."

The race was red-flagged for two hours, 38 minutes and 14 seconds while the fence was repaired.

"The fence did what it was supposed to do," said Bill France Jr., president of International Speedway Corp. and president of NASCAR.

During the winter, the original fence was replaced by a stronger one. "The old one was there for four races a year for 17 years, and a car never touched it," said Don Naman, who was the track's general manager.

During the break while the fence was fixed, Davey joined the Allison family in the ARCA garage where they spread their traditional picnic. Scarcely 30 minutes after the start of the race, with some 400 miles still to go, he was eating ham and potato salad.

"I sure hope I'm able to get back in that seat, fasten the belts and finish the race after all I've eaten," he said.

Unfortunately for the others, the belts fastened just fine.

1987

Bill Elliott's day ended where it began, but it was anything but dull. A crowd estimated at 105,000 saw the Dawsonville, GA, driver become only the second man to win the Talladega 500 from the pole position. Dave Marcis, in 1976, was the other one.

Elliott held off Davey Allison to win a remarkable eight-car dash to the finish after a mystery ailment earlier in the race had threatened to park his Melling Racing Ford.

The finale was set up by a caution period that ended with 34 laps to go. All the leaders had pitted and were ready to roll to the end.

Allison, who had led 77 of the 150 laps before the caution flag, got shuffled all the way back to eighth in the ensuing green-flag action. But he meticulously worked his way forward, and on lap 186 of the 188-lapper he passed Dale Earnhardt for second and was on Elliott's bumper.

As the last lap began, it was Elliott, Allison, Earnhardt, Cale Yarborough, Darrell Waltrip, Rusty Wallace, Terry Labonte and Lake Speed in that order, inches apart.

Allison tried to pass Elliott on the outside in the frontstretch dogleg, but Elliott faded high, and Davey couldn't make it. The margin of victory was 15/100ths of a second.

Earnhardt, Waltrip, Yarborough, Labonte, Speed and Wallace followed Allison, in that order.

Elliott wanted no part of laying back and attempting to slingshot another leader.

"I've always said up front was where I wanted to be with a group of cars running for it at the end," he explained. "I didn't want to take a chance of having to draft by the leader on the last lap.

"You've got to understand that with a lot of cars in the lead pack, second isn't necessarily where you want to be.

"The problem is that you think you're going to set the leader up, but then here comes somebody with nothing to lose to race you, and you're messed up."

Allison said he did his best, "but I couldn't get any closer to Bill on the last lap." He added, "That was the hardest I ever raced any time, anywhere, for any position.

"I had too much ground to make up there at the end. If I hadn't had to pass so many of them, maybe our car would have won the battle with the Thunderbirds."

Elliott's irregular route on the last lap kept Allison from drawing a bead. "I was trying to do anything I could to win, and I thought that was the thing to do," Elliott said.

Allison and most others took on four tires during the final caution, but Elliott got just two so that he could protect his track position. He was in front when the yellow period ended. He led the final 38 laps, which gave him 72 for the day.

He simply didn't want to be part of the melee behind the leader in the closing laps. "Davey got caught out of line once and went to the rear of the pack," Elliott pointed out. "If I had got hung out like Davey did I might not have got back. Besides, tires just aren't that crucial here."

With some 50 laps to go, Elliott's fans must have wondered if he would even finish the race, much less be in victory lane.

He swerved to miss another car in the pits, and the rear end of his racer "started chattering." He began losing ground on the track, but a propitious caution flag enabled him to pit twice for an exam.

"We thought we had a broken axle," Elliott said. "We pulled the right one, and it was okay. Then we pitted again to check the left one and didn't see anything. When we put it back in, the spring or whatever it was must have popped back into place. After that it was all right."

Elliott averaged 172.292 miles an hour in the second-fastest Talladega 500 in history, though NASCAR had mandated smaller carburetors at the track in view of Bobby Allison's crash into the catch fence in the Winston 500. Carburetor restrictor plates later would replace the smaller carburetors.

Of the eight drivers who sped cheek to cheek and jaw to jaw toward the checkered flag, three had won a Talladega 500, five had not. Elliott was one of the five, and so in the 19th Talladega 500 he became the 17th different winner.

Anyone with an ounce of compassion in his heart had to feel for the seven who came up feet short of victory.

"I just couldn't do anything with those Fords," the

Buddy Baker (88) was a strong challenger in the Talladega 500.

(above) Quick pit work helped Bill Elliott win the '87 Talladega 500.
(left) Alan Kulwicki debuted in the Zerex Ford for the '87 Winston 500.

Elliott is #1 after winning the '87 Talladega 500.

Chevy-driving Earnhardt said. The late laps "were just like a chess match."

Waltrip echoed the sentiment: "Those Fords were just so strong. The Fords were the thing. When you've got the two fastest cars in front, that's tough."

Racing with smaller carburetors was "a lot more fun," Waltrip said. "We don't have that 100 extra horsepower anymore, and you can't just blow somebody off by pressing the gas down," he added. "You've got to work your way by them."

Yarborough said his car was weak on the straightaway, and that his carburetor wasn't tuned perfectly. "I don't know how we could have beaten Elliott. I was in the draft and flat out. And on the last pit stop I got the slowest set of tires all day. Isn't that the way it goes?"

There were 22 lead changes among nine drivers, and Labonte led 22 laps, but the last one was 49 laps from the finish. "Earnhardt went by me going into the first turn, and I lost the draft," he said. "Everyone went by me, and I couldn't get back in line. With the new carburetor rules it's hard to break out and pass anyone."

Speed no doubt re-played the last laps in his mind for a few days.

"My car was so good I was going to be a hero and drive right to the front," he said. "When I pulled out, I went right to the back. When I finally quit trying to be a hero I was all right. I'm frustrated, that's all. To run so good all day, and then there at the end ..."

The stagger was off on his last set of tires, he said. "I hate to think where I finished. It makes me so sick."

Wallace shook his head. "I tried, I tried, I tried," he said. "I'd come by in fourth and fall back to eighth the next time by."

Allison was bidding for a sweep of Talladega's 1987 Winston Cup races, but it wasn't to be. "We went as hard as we could for as long as we could, and we just ran out of laps," he said. "Second is not a victory, but it beats third."

He got a nasty burn on his heel from exhaust heat. "I had it by the fifth lap," he said, "so it dealt me misery the entire race."

112

Talladega is an Indian word meaning "you'll never believe who's in victory lane this time." Not really. But the definition would be appropriate.

When young Phil Parsons won the 1988 Winston 500, he became the ninth Winston Cup driver to score his first superspeedway victory there. That was especially remarkable considering that it was just the 38th WC race at the track.

The others were Richard Brickhouse, James Hylton, Dick Brooks, Dave Marcis, Lennie Pond, Ron Bouchard, Bobby Hillin and Davey Allison.

When the first quarter-century of racing at Talladega ended in 1993, only two, Marcis and Allison, had ever won another Winston Cup event.

Parsons' previous claim to fame at the world's fastest track was that one of his racers was on permanent display in the museum of the International Motorsports Hall of Fame next door to the speedway. It did a spectacular barrel roll in the 1983 Winston 500, and it was displayed to illustrate the strength of a NASCAR roll cage. Parsons suffered only a broken shoulder and bruises.

Somebody was always asking him if he were afraid to get back on the world's biggest speedway.

"The next lap I ran at this track, I was comfortable," the Denver, NC, driver said firmly. "This is my favorite race track and always has been. I like to go fast, and this is the fastest of the fast."

A crowd estimated at 135,000 saw the 30-year-old brother of veteran Benny Parsons score his first Winston Cup victory of any kind in his 111th start. He beat Bobby Allison by three car lengths.

When he was a rookie five years before, he had predicted his first win would come at Talladega, and recently he had repeated the prediction. "It's been a long time coming," Parsons said after the deed was done. "Maybe the next one won't take so long."

Parsons and Geoff Bodine were the surprise dominators of the race. Bodine led 99 laps and Parsons 52. They fronted all but 37 of the 188 laps.

A late caution flag helped knock Bodine down to a third-place finish.

He and Parsons had established a 10.5-second lead over the field when Ricky Rudd's engine blew and the yellow waved on the 180th lap. When the green was displayed on 183, Allison had joined the party, and the trio left the rest of the competitors.

As the white flag was shown, Allison shot by Bodine. The 50-year-old Daytona 500 champion challenged Parsons, but he couldn't get around him.

"I just used my rearview mirror and went everywhere Bobby went," Parsons said.

Allison was taken to the infield hospital and treated for exhaustion. He was given oxygen and fluids. "One thing's for sure," he said. "I gave it all I had."

Parsons' wife, Marcia, and 4-month-old daughter Kinsley Rae accompanied him to the press box for the post-race interview. It was a nice touch that they shared his magic moment.

"The money hasn't crossed my mind," said Parsons when someone reminded him he had won $86,850 and was eligible for the Winston Million. "Obviously, it's nice to win what we won today and to have a shot at the $1 million, but the money just isn't that important.

"Words can't express how I feel," Parsons continued. "It's the most special feeling I've had since my little girl was born. I've wanted to do this since I was 5 years old."

Was there ever a time when he believed he might never get that first win?

"Not lately," the driver of the Jackson Brothers Oldsmobile answered. "Of course, there was a time when I was working 24 hours a day and wasn't seeming to get anywhere..."

Parsons wasn't cocky during the week leading up to the race, but for a man who had never won he seemed confident.

"Before we even came down here I knew we had a good chance to win the pole and the race," he said Sunday night. "We tested here before Easter, and I knew we had a good chance."

He didn't win the pole, but he qualified third. "I told myself this was the best shot we had ever had," he continued. "But what if we run good but lose a coil wire or

Bobby Allison leads the Talladega express.

(left) The lead pack mixes it up in the trioval.
(below) Dave Marcis makes a quick pit stop.

Phil Parsons enjoys his first Winston Cup victory.

something? Then people will forget all about us."

But his car and Bodine's were in a class by themselves, and each driver was patient, letting the other lead, and their two-car draft out-distanced the field. Parsons shot by Bodine on the 174th lap and never relinquished the lead again.

"We talked about it on the radio and decided I'd try to pass him with about 10 laps to go," Parsons said. "But with about 15 to go, Bodine started shuffling down the straightaway. I figured it was time to make my move around him.

"I didn't want to wait until there were four or five laps to go and there be a wreck and the caution come out."

Parsons said he was sorry to see the caution flag that allowed Allison to catch up "because I thought Geoff and I had the two best cars and that the race should be decided between the two of us.

"I hated to see Geoff not finish second because he had the second best car. Also, the caution flag meant I had those other cars to run against."

Even though it eventually led to him losing second place, Bodine said he was pleased when the final yellow was displayed because he felt he might be able to hook up in a draft with another car and shoot by Parsons.

"I couldn't do anything with Phil," Bodine said. "He was awful strong. I was hoping I could get someone behind me to push me along. If Allison had stayed with me and we had dropped back and taken a run at Parsons, we both could have passed him. But when Bobby made his move to pass me, that canceled that plan, and when Ken Schrader pulled alongside of me it really killed me."

Parsons' crew almost blew the race when it let him run out of gas a fourth of the way through. He didn't pit for fuel when the others did during a caution period. Then his tank ran dry, and he almost lost a lap during the subsequent green-flag stop. He was side by side with leader Schrader, who was trying to lap him, when Schrader spun out, and that produced another caution period that enabled Parsons to make up the ground.

Parsons kidded that he stayed on the track too long because he was in front, he didn't get up there often, and he couldn't bear to surrender the lead, but then he smiled and said, "No, we really were sleeping. We got caught asleep."

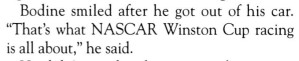

Talladega's summer race had a new name and a new title sponsor. Sears' DieHard brand of battery would back the DieHard 500.

But one thing hadn't changed. The speedway remained user-friendly to drivers not familiar with victory lane.

Ken Schrader of Fenton, MO, charged from fourth place on the last lap to score his first Winston Cup victory.

That enhanced the race's reputation as the zaniest on the planet, and the post-race inspection of his Chevrolet became another off-beat episode.

Winston Cup engines were limited to 358 cubic inches of displacement, but when Schrader's was checked immediately after the finish it measured 358.643. Would the winner be disqualified?

The rules allow for a three-hour cool down period if needed. After two hours Schrader's engine had shrunk to 357.980. He was home free.

It was a great race that featured a classic final lap, one on which Schrader made up for a boner that could have cost him victory.

"We were in the hunt with 20 laps to go," he explained, "and I made one of my brilliant superspeedway moves and got back to 13th place, and it took me 20 laps to get back up there.

"I was fourth, and I thought third looked better and pulled out of line. When I got back in line I was 13th.

"I learned a lot racing here in May, but with 20 laps to go I forgot it all. Then I remembered it again."

Veteran crew chief Harry Hyde coached Schrader over the radio. "Harry kept hollering for me to get back up there so we could worry about winning the race," Schrader said. "And then, with two laps to go, I realized I was back in. Finally, I went from fourth to first, which is the way things happen at Talladega."

When the white flag waved, Dale Earnhardt was leading, Geoff Bodine was second, Sterling Marlin was third, Schrader was fourth, Rick Wilson was fifth and five others were locked in a 10-car draft.

Schrader moved to the outside in the first turn, and Wilson tagged onto his bumper. That aerodynamic hookup helped propel Schrader into the lead. He held it and beat Bodine by a car length as Bodine and Earnhardt finished side by side, Geoff getting second and Dale third.

Wilson was fourth.

"Sterling and Dale touched, and it took four or five seconds for Dale to save his life, and we trucked on," the effusive Schrader said. "When Sterling and Dale got together, that was the break we needed."

It didn't really take four or five seconds, but it did throw Earnhardt off stride.

"I don't know what Sterling was doing," Earnhardt said. "He hit me four or five times. I thought he was going to spin me out. Geoff was trying to keep Sterling behind, then Sterling got rough with me. He finally had me going sideways."

Marlin shrugged it off. "Every man for himself," he said. "I tried Earnhardt on the outside, and he came across. So I went to the inside, and he was there. It's a situation where you take no prisoners on the last lap. He'd have done the same thing."

Bodine smiled after he got out of his car. "That's what NASCAR Winston Cup racing is all about," he said.

He didn't get the chance to make a move on Earnhardt on the backstretch, as he had planned. "They jumped out of line sooner than I wanted to," Bodine said, "and I had to try some new strategy after that. Schrader would make a move, but I couldn't do anything to block it."

Rusty Wallace, who finished fifth, pronounced it "the damnedest finish I've ever seen. We wrecked for a solid lap and got away with it."

Schrader led only eight laps, and he might never have been in victory lane if Darrell Waltrip's car had lasted. Waltrip led 123 of the 188 circuits and had the fastest machine, but its camshaft broke after 162 laps.

"It really is frustrating," Waltrip said. "It was the fastest car I ever drove. It was the strongest car of all time. It could do anything, any time."

A crowd estimated at 90,000 on a brutally hot day saw Schrader become the 18th different winner in 20 editions of the summer classic.

The 33-year-old Schrader had pulled to the line 107 times over five seasons without a win, but No. 1 had to come soon, because he had landed a ride with one of the rich Hendrick Motorsports teams, and the brilliant 64-

Pit road is a busy place during the DieHard 500.

(above) Davey Allison, Darrell Waltrip and company look for the green flag.
(left) Darrell Waltrip led for most of the race.

119

Ken Schrader won the first DieHard-sponsored race at Talladega.

year-old Harry Hyde was his crew chief.

Schrader drove Junie Donlavey's under-funded car the season before, and if he had been in it on this day he might not have stuck its nose where it had to go to find victory.

"The biggest thing we've fought all year is that I was used to just making laps," Schrader admitted. "That was the kind of budget Junie had.

"Last year, we would have been looking at a fourth- or fifth-place finish and bringing the car back in one piece. But this time it was win the race or maybe lose the car. I've had to learn to drive like that."

It was Schrader's first victory, but it was Hyde's 56th. "Back in February I told you I wouldn't trade him for anybody I knew," Harry told the press.

Both Hyde and Schrader described the driver as a man who thinks only of racing. That trait was evident as he reflected on his win at Talladega. It was the biggest, richest victory of his career, of course, but he wouldn't rank it over another one as far as producing a pure thrill.

"It's super to win here," he said, "but in 1978 or 1979, on July 4, I won a USAC midget race and got $300. I had been trying for three years to win one of those

things. This is just on another level."

Schrader became the 10th Winston Cup driver to score his first superspeedway win at Talladega. It was the 39th WC race at the track. He couldn't find victory lane when it was over. He drove off down the wrong road. "I just didn't want to quit yet," he said.

Nineteen cars finished on the lead lap, a record for the Winston Cup circuit. The old mark was 17 in the 1988 Daytona 500.

The heat of the day was so overbearing that several on-board fire extinguishers discharged during the race. Rodney Combs, Morgan Shepherd, Greg Sacks, Phil Parsons and Ken Bouchard all had their cars filled with the powdered mixture while at racing speeds.

The most untimely release came in Phil Parsons' racer. The winner of the 1988 Winston 500 had worked himself into fourth place when his extinguisher went off eight laps from the end. He fell behind and finished 11th.

"I couldn't see a thing and had to get off the gas a little," Parsons said. "It's hard to drive 190-some miles an hour and not be able to see."

1989

Davey Allison did what every boy loves to do: show off for his daddy. With the injured Bobby Allison watching from one of the VIP suites, Davey held off Terry Labonte and Mark Martin to win the Winston 500 before an estimated 140,000 fans.

"I can't wait to see him," Davey said of his father. "This is the first race he's been to that we won since he was injured at Pocono. He's been to several, but not that we won."

On Feb. 14, 1988, Bobby won the Daytona 500 with Davey finishing second, two car lengths behind. It was the beginning of what surely would be a wonderful season for the Allison family.

But it didn't turn out that way. On June 19, 1988, Bobby was grievously injured in a crash in a race at Pocono. A long, tedious, painful period of recovery was ahead for the veteran from Hueytown, AL.

On July 31, 1988, while the DieHard 500 was being run, Bobby was dismissed from Lehigh Valley Hospital in Allentown, PA, flown to Birmingham and admitted to Lakeshore Rehabilitation Hospital.

His return was kept secret until it was announced at the DieHard 500.

"The doctors were satisfied with Bobby's recovery and felt it was time for him to return to Alabama," his wife Judy explained in a prepared statement.

"We moved today because Bobby's physical condition was strong enough to allow it. We also felt any media coverage or a highly visible or public return to Alabama would not aid his recovery at this time."

Bobby eventually returned to the Winston Cup circuit as a car owner. In the next to last event of the first quarter-century of racing at Talladega, his driver, Jimmy Spencer, finished second.

Bobby's crash was one in a series of numbing tragedies that would strike the Allison family. Bobby and Judy's son, Clifford, was killed in a wreck while practicing at Michigan in August of 1992, and 11 months later, in July of 1993, Davey was fatally injured in a helicopter crash at Talladega Superspeedway.

That was the name of the track when the 1989 Winston 500 rolled off. No longer was it Alabama International Motor Speedway, the name it had carried since it opened in 1969. With the Talladega 500 becoming the DieHard 500, officials wanted to keep "Talladega" before the public, so they changed the name of the arena. Besides, everyone referred to the speedway simply as "Talladega," anyway.

"This is my home track," Davey said after his victory. "All my family and friends are here, not to mention that we've won some races at this speedway. We needed to focus on Talladega, and we did. For instance, in our testing we spent an entire day working on the qualifying setup. We had never done that before, anywhere."

The focus paid off, for the victory lane cameras were focused on Davey after he beat Labonte by 22/100ths of a second in one of those patented Talladega last-lap thrillers.

It was his first win of the season, and it ended a 14-race drought dating back to September of the year before. With two Winston Cup victories and four ARCA wins, he was Talladega Superspeedway's winningest driver. The source of his knack for getting around the huge track? "If I knew the answer to that question I wouldn't tell anybody," came the predictable reply.

The audience was liberally sprinkled with members of the huge Allison clan and, of course, Davey was the favorite of many Alabamans.

"This has been an up and down season, but this is the greatest place to turn it around," he said.

He was well armed for the turnaround. "This was a brand new race car," the Hueytown driver said. "It drove perfect. All I had to do was steer it and mash the gas."

Robert Yates was the man behind the car. A year before he was the team's crew chief. Now he was crew chief and owner. Rich Harry Ranier sold it to him, and in the Winston 500, Yates got his first victory as the boss.

"I just wondered if we were ever going to do it," Yates said. "It's good to get the first win of a season, and it's good to win a race without the support of a wealthy man."

Davey's Ford was the strongest car in the race. It led 94 of the 188 laps, but he had to work for the victory.

Morgan Shepherd was leading and Allison was second when a crash involving at least nine cars occurred in the

The leaders chase winner, Davey Allison.

(above) Rick Wilson leads a group into the high banks.
(left) Labonte leads the field en route to a second place finish.

Davey Allison captures his second Winston 500.

fourth turn on lap 172 . The green waved on lap 177, and the last chase of the bright, sunny day was on.

Allison dogged Shepherd and finally passed him on lap 180 in the 27th and final lead change of the day. Allison, Labonte and Martin pulled away, and it became a three-man duel.

Labonte, riding on Davey's bumper, ducked low in the frontstretch dogleg on the last lap, but Ernie Irvan's lapped car was there. Labonte moved high, but he didn't have the oomph to pass Davey.

Was Davey certain he had the horses to beat Terry?

"I didn't know whether I had the power or not," he said, "but I made sure I was in the place they wanted to be in. I wasn't going to do anything stupid, but I was sure going to protect that lead."

Where did he expect Labonte to make his move?

"Anywhere," Davey answered. "I don't think I looked out the windshield the whole last lap. I know this place by heart, so I can drive it with the mirror.

"If they were going to make a move anywhere on the track there were going to be three cars going that way, not two."

Labonte said he did all he could do. "I think Davey was holding back today. We couldn't do anything with him. Mark Martin couldn't do anything with me, and I couldn't do anything with Davey. It was a good run for us, though."

Martin started on the pole and Davey on the outside of the front row, but Davey's car clearly was superior in the race.

"We weren't strong enough," Martin said. "We were there, but we didn't have anything for Davey at the end.

"Terry and I were doing this and that, trying to get something up," he explained, demonstrating hand signals, "but when the time came, we couldn't even get up to Davey. The way Davey was running, nobody was going to beat him."

It was an uncanny day for Davey Allison. "It seemed like the holes kept opening for me, and I'd be able to pass and get back in line," he said. "It's hard to explain. Something would happen, like somebody would get loose and the others would back off, and that would be when I was making my move, and I'd have a hole to drop into."

Chevrolet debuted its 1990 Lumina in the race, but Fords took the top three positions.

Joe Willie Namath called his shot, and Babe Ruth supposedly did, too. Why shouldn't Darrell Waltrip get into the act?

Asked who was going to win the DieHard 500, Waltrip replied flatly: "We are."

He had reasons. "We're running really good, and when my car runs good here I can run the kind of race I want to. We know we're in good shape when we qualify good. When we qualify well, we run well. We're pretty confident."

As far as Davey Allison was concerned, Waltrip could have the favorite's role. Allison was generally considered the likely winner, but when he was asked if he should be favored he answered, "No. Why should I be?"

Maybe because he won the Winston 500 at Talladega and the Pepsi 400 at Daytona, two races run with carburetor restrictors, as the DieHard 500 would be.

"So what?" Allison replied. "This is the DieHard 500, the most unpredictable race. There shouldn't be a favorite. The favorite rarely wins."

He knew his history. There had been 20 of the summer classics and 18 different victors.

Why had there been just two repeat winners?

"I'll tell you one reason, and it's simple," said Waltrip. "Nobody ever even thinks about it, but it's simple. It's because of where the start-finish line is."

Waltrip pointed to the stripe near the end of the front straightaway. "If the start-finish line were back here in the middle of the dogleg like it is everywhere else, then the same guy would have won this race four or five times. I would have won it about three more times, because I was leading at that point in more than a few other occasions.

"But the location of the start-finish line and the width of the dogleg has a lot to do with it. You can't fend off everybody. You can block one guy, but you can't block two or three.

"When they come through here and get three or four wide, you never know who's going to win.

"The other thing is that it's an easy race track to win on. Guys find themselves in a position to win here when they never have before because it's an easy track to drive.

"If you can survive the early going and be there at the finish, then it's potluck."

But Waltrip didn't win the 1989 DieHard 500, and neither did Allison. Terry Labonte won it, while Darrell finished second and Davey ninth.

The Corpus Christi, TX, driver took the lead from Waltrip on lap 176 of the 188-lapper and held him off to win by half a car length.

Apparently adhering to the theory of leave while you're still in love, Labonte announced in victory lane that he would depart Junior Johnson's Ford team and form a team with himself as driver in 1990.

Labonte confirmed rumors of a split-up. "I just thought this would be a good time to say it," he explained later. "I've been dodging a lot of questions. I haven't lied to anybody, but I've brushed them off."

Was he leaving on his own accord or had Johnson asked him to leave? "We've never even discussed it," Labonte answered.

He was in his third year as Johnson's driver, but the DieHard 500 was only the fourth win their union had produced.

It was Labonte's first victory at Talladega Superspeedway and he became the 19th different winner in 21 of the summer races. Three times he had finished second at the world's fastest track, but his most memorable near miss was in the 1981 Talladega 500 when he and Waltrip and Ron Bouchard came across the line side by side in a photo finish. Bouchard won and Labonte was third.

"I'd rather win a race here than anywhere because I've been so close so many times," Labonte said when he finally earned the pomp of victory lane. "When I came across the finish line I said, 'I don't believe it.' I still don't believe it."

Waltrip made a final effort toward the inside near the end, but his car didn't have the power to complete the move.

"I think about all Waltrip could do was stay where he was," Labonte said. "The draft doesn't work as good as it used to, and the lead is the place to be on the last lap. These cars are so aerodynamic that they don't make a big hole in the wind, so it's hard to slingshot by anybody

Labonte edged Martin (6), Waltrip (17) and Schrader (25) for the victory.

(above) Drivers prepare for the green flag.
(left) Darrell Waltrip led eight times during the '89 DieHard.

Terry Labonte and Junior Johnson are all smiles after winning the '89 DieHard 500.

anymore."

The cars of Labonte, Waltrip, Mark Martin, Ken Schrader, Rick Wilson, Morgan Shepherd and Allison had broken out of the pack in a lead draft when Davey's racer spun out on the 181st lap. That brought out a caution, and after the green waved on 184 Labonte and Waltrip pulled away from the others.

"I looked in the mirror, and all I could see was Darrell behind me," Labonte said. "Then I saw the rest of them farther back. I guess Darrell and I got lined up, and they got to racing each other side by side, and that let us get away."

Said Waltrip: "Things really got sticky on that last restart. I couldn't take a chance of me and Terry messing up and getting side by side and dragging everybody else into the race. It was better to race one guy and take your chances than it was to race the rest of that bunch behind us.

"I thought Terry and I might end up with a photo finish, but it didn't quite work out that way.

"If I could have jumped him on the restart I would have been the winner, and he would have finished second. But it didn't happen that way.

"I thought I had something for him there at the end, but he was just too strong for me. I tried to go everywhere and make a move on him, but nothing worked."

Labonte felt good about his chances on Saturday and better about them Sunday morning.

"I thought yesterday during practice that the car was capable of winning," he said. "You notice we didn't practice much. We thought it was real good, and we didn't want to wear it out.

"Then this morning they told me my brother Bobby won on the short track at Concord, NC, Saturday night. It seems like every time he wins on Saturday, I win on Sunday."

It was the fifth-straight victory for Ford. "The new Fords really work good on the big tracks," Labonte said. "but we need to get them dialed in on the short tracks and the road courses."

Ken Schrader led as late as the 172nd lap—but his pregnant wife Ann wasn't looking. She finally had to turn away and sit against the fence on the back of pit row where she couldn't see what was going on.

"I can't stand to watch," she said. "I've been praying all week on this one."

He finished fourth, and his $28,500 pay day would buy a lot of diapers.

There were 49 lead changes among 10 drivers. Shepherd led 70, Labonte led 25 and Waltrip 32.

There was a Hollywood beginning to the Winston 500, but Dale Earnhardt saw that there would be no Hollywood ending.

Moviemakers spent much of the 1990 season at NASCAR races, shooting a film called Days of Thunder. It starred Tom Cruise. Cruise always liked the first name Cole, and a producer or somebody was captivated by Dick Trickle's last name. Hence, the birth of Cole Trickle, midwifed by the stroke of a scriptwriter's pen.

Greg Sacks did the driving for Cruise. The Cole Trickle kissing the girls was Tom Cruise; the Cole Trickle kissing the wall was Greg Sacks. Greg did not have a regular ride on the Winston Cup circuit, so he was free to make a movie.

Charlotte businessman Rick Hendrick furnished Cole Trickle's car, and when most of the shooting was done he and actor Paul Newman decided to turn the play-like team into a real one. They were co-owners of the car that made its debut in the Winston 500, with Sacks driving. Hendrick already owned a stableful of teams; what was one more?

Paramount mopped up its filming in the Winston 500. It shot the pace lap and some crowd scenes.

Before the 500 started, Sacks chatted about his part-time job. "I haven't been in racing week in and week out like most of these guys this season. I've been busy working with the movie—which has been a blast—but I don't think I'm rusty. When you get back to the track, it's like you never left."

Life imitates art. Sacks drove his car into the lead draft, in his best imitation of Cole Trickle, and kept it there all day. He wasn't rusty at all.

One by one hosses dropped from contention until only Earnhardt and Sacks were left. The last lap began with Greg on Dale's bumper.

But this wasn't make believe. It was for real, and there would be no Hollywood finish. Cole Trickle (a.k.a. Greg Sacks) couldn't pass the man they call the Intimidator.

There was awe in Sacks' voice when he said, "We came up on the lapped car of Bill Elliott, and Bill got down in the dirt to let us by, and Dale followed him right down into the dirt to pick up his draft and get an extra pull."

Richard Childress, owner of the winning Chevrolet, spoke a perfect testimonial:

"When you've got Dale Earnhardt in your car at the end, you've got something extra."

Hendrick, who also fielded cars for Darrell Waltrip, Ken Schrader and Ricky Rudd, wasn't shocked by Sacks' fine finish.

"When Sacks unloaded here, he had one of the quickest cars," Hendrick said. "It drove good, it was good aerodynamically, and I knew he was going to be aggressive, so his performance didn't surprise me. Some other crew chiefs told me the car was a rocket, so I knew we had something."

Earnhardt led the final 22 laps to score his third Winston Cup victory at Talladega as a crowd estimated at 140,000 looked on. The Mooresville, NC, driver finished two lengths ahead of Sacks. Well behind the leaders came Mark Martin.

Earnhardt led 113 of the 188 laps as he celebrated the first anniversary of Chevrolet's Lumina race car. The Lumina debuted in the 1989 Winston 500. Earnhardt's victory a year later gave it 13 wins in 30 races for a solid .433 percentage.

"Our hat's off to Greg Sacks," Earnhardt said. "He was the one I was worried about. When he wanted to go to the front, it seemed he could.

"When it came down to a two-car race between us, I was watching him in my mirror. It seemed he fell off in the corners and would make a good run on the straightaways. So I started falling off in the corners. I was working him as much as he was working me. We were both feeling each other out.

"He was laying back a little, and on the last lap I pulled away coming out of the second turn more than he expected. I was also helped by Elliott's draft.

"We raced into three and four, and I closed the door on him."

Sacks simply didn't have the oomph to pass Earnhardt on the frontstretch.

"I was just waiting for the last lap," he said. "I felt like the best move for me was to stay even through turn No. 4 and then make my move. I laid back and tried to make a

Derrike Cope hoped to win the second leg of the Winston million.

(above) Bill Elliott's team gives him quick service in pit row.
(left) A huge crowd enjoys the side-by-side racing.

Earnhardt wound up in victory lane after beating Sacks.

move on him.

"It was a little cat and mouse game there at the end.

"I rolled the dice, but they came up snake eyes."

But Sacks was smiling as he walked through the garage, his arm draped around the shoulders of his crew chief, Gary Dehart.

"We did okay for the first time, didn't we?" Sacks offered. "It's a great car. Gary built it from the ground up for the movie. It was really great today."

Sacks led 35 laps and Ken Schrader 20 laps. Schrader spent much of the afternoon running with Earnhardt and Sacks, but on the 149th lap he pulled behind the pit wall to fix a distributor problem.

"I'm disappointed," said Schrader's crew chief, Richard Broome. "We were looking for a pretty good run there at the end, but it was just one of those deals that wasn't meant to be."

Also disappointed was Elliott, who started on the pole but never led a lap. "My day wasn't worth a flip," said Elliott, who experienced a series of misfortunes.

Stunned might be a better word than disappointed for Derrike Cope, the surprise winner of the 1990 Daytona 500 who was looking forward to the tour's stop at Daytona International Speedway's sister track, Talladega Superspeedway, in his quest for the Winston Million. Cope lasted only three laps before his engine failed.

"The timing backed up," he explained. "We had the same problem in practice yesterday. It was running real good, just sitting there relaxing, and the motor backed up and started coming apart."

It was the same engine that carried him to victory at Daytona.

"We ran over a rabbit on the backstretch during practice Thursday, but I guess four rabbit's feet aren't as lucky as one," Cope said. "Racing luck is strange. I finished first at Daytona, and I was the first one out of the race today. Disappointment is a big part of racing, but you've just got to shake your head and keep going."

Said third-placer Martin: "There were about 10 or 12 cars that could really run today, and the rest of the field weren't able to hang on.

"I tell you, Sacks could push Earnhardt so fast in the draft that I don't think anybody could keep up with them. There were a few times I could hang onto them, but I mean it was dear life. When they decided to go, they left the rest of us."

1990

On the morning of the DieHard 500, a newspaper column said that Dale Earnhardt would win the race. There were no ifs, no maybes, no hedging. The writer stated flatly that Earnhardt would win.

Dale was so strong, so obviously superior to the rest of the field, that he inspired that kind of confidence.

Two days before the 500, Bobby Allison, owner of the car Hut Stricklin would drive, summed up the case for making Earnhardt the favorite: "When you've got the best team and the best driver in racing, you've got a pretty good head start."

Richard Childress, Earnhardt's car owner, was as comfortable on the hot seat as an Eskimo on a block of ice. Asked if his team should be favored, he replied: "Yeah. We've won two of the three at tracks with the carburetor restrictor this year, and without the tire problem in the Daytona 500 we'd be three for three."

Earnhardt dominated the Daytona 500 only to finish fifth when he ran over debris on the final lap. He won the Winston 500 at Talladega Superspeedway and the Pepsi 400 at Daytona.

Childress never won as a driver, but as a car owner he proved himself a genius at assembling a winning organization.

"The opportunity came along nine years ago today, and I took it," Childress said on Friday before the DieHard 500. "That's when I got a top sponsor and a top driver. It was right over there in the Downtowner in Anniston."

Wrangler was the sponsor, and Earnhardt was the driver. Earnhardt switched to Bud Moore's team for the 1982 and 1983 seasons before returning to Childress in 1984, and Goodwrench eventually replaced Wrangler, but over the seasons the team delivered on the promise implicit in the signing of those first contracts.

Childress, Earnhardt and the supporting cast were cut from the old cloth that was woven when stock car racing was more of a game than a business.

"The money doesn't play nearly as big a part as wanting to win," Childress said. "I'd give back all the money we got for the Daytona 500 for the winner's trophy."

For the record, that was $109,325.

"Winning drives this team," Childress continued. "I don't know exactly how to say it, but we don't like to see others win. You've got to always leave mad when you don't win."

Childress could look into his garage stall at Talladega Superspeedway and see a crew that had been together for years. "I hire people like Dale and me—who want to win, not just have a job—and I try to put enough incentive in there that they'll want to stay," he said. "I don't hire them all from racing, either. I might hire a man from a car dealership. I get five or six applications a week, and if I see something I like, I put it back."

And Childress could see a driver who was at the top of his game, old enough to have the experience, young enough to have the verve. "I think he's the best driver out there," Childress said.

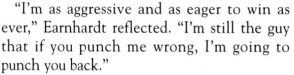

"I'm as aggressive and as eager to win as ever," Earnhardt reflected. "I'm still the guy that if you punch me wrong, I'm going to punch you back."

But he said conducting rookie meetings had led him to discretion. "You've got to back off sometimes. You preach all these things to the rookies and you start trying to set an example for them."

The other drivers' fears were answered in the DieHard 500. Earnhardt led 134 of the 188 laps, an event record, and won his sixth race of 1990. His payday of $152,975 included the $68,000 Unocal Challenge, given for winning the pole and the race.

Earnhardt's Chevrolet thus led 1,343 of the 1,900 miles at Daytona and Talladega, the two tracks that required carburetor restrictors.

When he was not leading the DieHard 500, Earnhardt seemed insulted. Early in the race, though he clearly had everyone covered, he bolted through the traffic as if he were trying to get to the boat before the ferry closed for the night.

Earnhardt's crew chief, Kirk Shelmerdine, was awed. "Man, those holes have got to be wider than they look from down here," he said as the Mooresville, NC, driver darted in and out of the procession.

Earnhardt displayed remarkable restraint—for a

Richard Petty relaxes before the race.

(left) Earnhardt maneuvers in heavy traffic.
(below) Ernie Irvan emerged as a strong
DieHard contender.

Earnhardt is back in victory lane.

while—late in the race. Bill Elliott led 18 laps, and Earnhardt was on his bumper, drafting to conserve fuel. Finally, he could stand it no longer, and he fired around Elliott to lead the final 10.

Their skirmish provided a one-act drama on an otherwise cut-and-dried afternoon—but even the most devout Elliott fans among an estimated 90,000 on hand must have sensed that Earnhardt could take him whenever he wanted to.

"He let me lead for a while," Elliott put it. "He was just messing around."

Childress told Earnhardt to draft Elliott. Lap after lap, the impatient Earnhardt asked for permission to shoot down the leader. "I never told him to pass Bill," Childress explained later. "After he did, he asked me if it was all right. I said, 'Well, yeah, I guess it is.' I was going to tell him to go within another lap or two. Dale just doesn't like to run second."

Earnhardt had made a mockery of the other drivers' complaints that they couldn't pass at Talladega and Daytona because of the carburetor restrictor. He passed them at will.

"With the restrictor, you have to work the air and the draft and make the car pull freer," Earnhardt said in the post-race press conference.

"I learned drafting from guys like Buddy Baker and Bobby Allison and Donnie Allison and Cale Yarborough. I got beat by a lot by them. The experience of knowing the draft is the answer to the restrictor.

"I did it just right to get by Bill Elliott. And I'm not going to give those secrets away, either."

Earnhardt missed running the fastest DieHard 500 ever by mere seconds, averaging 174.429 miles an hour. The fastest at that time was in 1978, when Lennie Pond won at 174.700.

"I just didn't want to be behind anybody," said Earnhardt. "I got a cramp in my right foot going wide open all day, and my big toe got burnt from sticking it to the firewall."

Terry Labonte, who won the 1989 DieHard 500, finished last in the '90 DieHard, his engine broken after just six laps. "I've got an oil leak in the oil pan and water coming out of the tail pipe," Labonte said as his crew hovered around his car. "It doesn't look good."

Such are the fortunes of racing.

It is generally accepted that at a stock car race the heroes are on the track. But there were plenty in the grandstands and infield at the Winston 500. No flashy, dramatic heroes. Just everyday folks making the best of a bad situation, hanging in there like a rusty fish hook.

On Saturday, the customers put up with four hours and 15 minutes of rain delays to watch the preliminary races.

An estimated 130,000 spectators were in the speedway Sunday when the rains returned. A deluge straight out of Genesis struck the track, and high winds caused the press box to be evacuated.

Fans couldn't have been wetter if they had plunged into nearby Lake Logan Martin. The parking lot was an ocean of mud. Vehicles were stuck up to their axles.

One poor fellow, thinking he was eyeing surface water, drove ahead—and into a low area where the water covered all but the top of his car.

Folks tried to help folks. They tugged at stuck cars, and they offered shelter and whatever assistance they could. They were shirtless and shoeless and muddy, and they laughed at their predicament because they had to laugh to keep from crying.

The 1991 Winston 500 became only the second Winston Cup race ever to be rained out at Talladega. The 1977 Winston 500 was postponed a week.

But 1991 was the fourth year of NASCAR's "next clear day" policy, and the race was set for Monday.

Monday morning was rainy and foggy but, incredibly, an estimated 105,000 presented their rain checks. They put up with another rain delay of an hour and 45 minutes before the Winston 500 finally was birthed.

If racing audiences are largely blue-collar, it was appropriate that a blue-collar driver, Harry Gant, won the event.

Gant had made $5 million racing, and he often was referred to by the media as a former carpenter, but that wasn't true. He was an active carpenter.

"I try to do three months' worth a year," he said in the post-race interview. "Of course, it's two days here, two days there. I'm building two garages now. When I get through with them I'll start another building. I built a house for one of my daughters, and I'm going to build a house for another one."

When Gant won at Pocono in 1990, he was 50 years and 158 days old. He replaced Bobby Allison as the oldest man ever to win a Winston Cup race. He gilded his record in the Winston 500. In fact, the Taylorsville, NC, driver was the oldest man to win any 500-mile race.

"It doesn't seem like you're 51," Gant said. "You're out there racing, and you feel like 30. Age doesn't have a lot to do with it."

Gant got a late start in Winston Cup. He was 39 when he attacked the circuit regularly, in 1979. He finished second to Dale Earnhardt in the Rookie of the Year chase.

Gant was a teen-aged terror behind the wheel of a passenger car. He'd race all challengers from Dog Crossing to  Paul Payne's store. He was like the gunfighter everybody had to challenge. But it wasn't until 1964, after he was married and working in his family's construction business, that he drove on a track, in a hobby car race.

He became a nationally prominent Sportsman driver, and in 1979, an owner named Jack Beebe figured Gant could handle a Winston Cup car. Harry paid his own expenses to get the ride, sleeping in his van to save motel money.

In 1981 movie actor Burt Reynolds and stuntman Hal Needham put him in their car, and his career soared.

Gant won the Winston 500 by getting superior gas mileage. He watched from behind while Darrell Waltrip and Dale Earnhardt tried to out-rabbit each other. The result was that he made one less pit stop than they did, and that won the trophy for him.

"It was hard not to go up there and run with them," he said, "but the pits kept telling me on the radio, 'Don't do it! Don't do it! Save gas! Save gas!'"

Gant said his engine began "stinking" on the last lap, that it shut off at about the beginning of the frontstretch dogleg, and that he coasted across the finish line. He guessed that a piston was burned. He still beat Waltrip by 14 seconds.

Gant's victory was a controversial one, though. Two hours after the fans had gone home thinking he was the winner, he wasn't so sure, and neither were several other

The late Alan Kulwicki reflects before the Winston.

(above) Ricky Rudd checks his Tide Chevrolet before the Winston.
(left) A wreck on the backstretch left some cars short on sheet metal.

Gant and crew acknowledge cheers following his Winston 500 victory.

interested parties.

NASCAR officials reviewed TV tapes to see if Gant's No. 33 got an illegal push from Rick Mast's No. 1 when Gant seemed to run out of gas on the final lap. Rules state that a car cannot be pushed on the last lap.

"The No. 33 was tapped by the No. 1 car coming down the backstretch," said Dick Beaty, the Winston Cup director. "We removed the fuel cell and all the hoses from the 33 car and found about a quart of gasoline left. We felt that was sufficient fuel for him to finish the race without help."

Beaty also said the spoiler angle on Waltrip's car was less than the required 30 degrees, but that NASCAR erred in not checking it on pit road, so the order of finish would stand.

Gant's Oldsmobile was owned by Leo Jackson, and Mast's Oldsmobile was owned by his brother Richard Jackson, and they had the same sponsor.

Gant said Mast's car bumped his but didn't push it. The brothers, he said, are rivals who "want to beat each other more than anybody" and that there was no communication between the two teams during the race.

"He got a little loose up there in three and four," Mast said. "It messed his car up, and I bumped him pretty hard. If I did help him, so be it. Keep it all in the family."

Mast added: "I didn't get any orders from the pits. The radio went down with two laps to go."

Waltrip said there was no question Mast pushed Gant. "Let's be realistic. Everybody saw it. He's out of gas. Here's a guy back there nine laps down helping him. What did he have to lose?"

Davey Allison said, "Mast pushed him all the way down the backstretch and again in three and four."

Earnhardt couldn't pass Waltrip for second on the final circuit. "Darrell had too much for me on the last lap," he said. "I couldn't do anything with him. I was going to race him for second, but I couldn't catch him."

As if all the rain delays weren't enough, there was a 20-car crash on the 71st lap, and the race was stopped for 33 minutes and 32 seconds. Kyle Petty suffered a compound fracture of the thighbone.

Gant smelled the crash coming. He didn't like the way a couple of men were driving, but he wouldn't name them. "We had dropped way back," he said. "I told the crew something was going to happen."

1991

The Fords of Davey Allison, Bill Elliott and Sterling Marlin hooked up in a draft in an attempt to beat Dale Earnhardt's Chevrolet in the closing laps of the DieHard 500.

The way Richard Childress saw it, that just made the sides even.

"I think we had the evening factor with Dale," said Earnhardt's car owner. "He's good, and now he's won five times here. He knows what it takes to win. This was his best—and the most exciting."

A crowd estimated at 100,000 saw Earnhardt beat Elliott by a car length. That gave the Mooresville, NC, driver three wins in the most recent four races at Talladega. He had won the DieHard 500 four times and the Winston 500 once to become the track's leading victor in Winston Cup races. He had been tied at four with Bobby Allison, Buddy Baker and Darrell Waltrip.

"I like to set records," Earnhardt said. "It's another mark in your book, another piece of history in your career."

There were 32 lead changes among 12 drivers, but Earnhardt led 101 of the 188 laps.

It was a magnificent race, It never lagging under green. The leader was always hounded. And there were enough caution flags—seven—to keep the pack bunched.

"In a race like this, you're looking behind you about as much as you're looking in front of you," Earnhardt commented paying tribute to the 500.

There was an oddity that the fans didn't see, a confession by Ernie Irvan, who wanted to ditch his nickname of Swervin' Irvan.

In the pre-race drivers' meeting, Irvan stood and told the others: "I've driven a little over-aggressive at times this season, and I've lost the respect of a lot of drivers and car owners in this garage area. That really hurts me. "I'm going to work on being more patient, and I hope you'll give me the chance to prove it and gain that respect back."

Irvan had tapped leader Hut Stricklin and spun him out at Pocono the week before.

Alas, Irvan was involved in a big wreck in the DieHard 500. His car shot up the track in the first turn, and then it and nine others were brawling.

"We got tapped from behind," Irvan said. "I don't know who it was. It was one of those deals, and there's not much you can do about it.

"I think he was trying to get in the bottom lane, but I was already there. It's one of those racing incidents."

Buddy Baker said he believed the accident was triggered when one of Irvan's tires went down.

The most spectacular crash of the day—one of the most spectacular ever at the speedway, considering its location—happened when Rick Mast's car went into a 500-yard skid on its roof on the frontstretch.

Mast scrambled out, waved to the fans in the grandstand, then made a joke to the press: "I'm okay, except I might need a new pair of britches after getting upside down like that."

Baker's car, he said, "got up underneath me and got me sideways, and that was all she wrote. It wasn't really his fault. We were just racing.

"I'll tell you, though, the first thing you think is 'please stop,' and then you think 'please don't anybody hit me while I'm sitting here,' and then you think 'please don't catch fire while I'm trying to get out of here.'

"I'll tell you, my heart was beating about 300 times a minute."

The 1-2 Earnhardt-Elliott finish was a repeat of the one in the 1990 DieHard 500. After a caution period, the race boiled down to a six-lap chase under green.

The Fords of Marlin, Allison and Elliott hooked up nose to tail to rip past the fourth-, third- and second-place cars and zoom in on leader Earnhardt.

But with three laps to go, the Ford brotherhood dissolved when Allison made the first move to challenge Earnhardt and nobody followed him.

Allison pulled out on the backstretch and got his car alongside the leader's, but he was stranded out of line and, out of the draft, he dropped back to an eventual ninth-place finish.

"All we needed was four more inches and we could have moved up in front of Earnhardt, and had him," said

The intimidator, Dale Earnhardt leads the way.

(above) The King pits for a tire change.
(left) Earnhardt earns another DieHard trophy.

Earnhardt (3), Spencer (98) and Allison (28) battle for the lead.

Allison. "That's all we needed, four more inches.

"I got hung out there. When you don't have any draft help, nobody there to push you, you can't do it. We ended up back there in the pack getting cracked by other people."

Allison was furious with Marlin. He climbed from his racer and sprinted to his car hauler, pausing only to slam his fist into a wooden door—fracturing his hand in the process.

That left Elliott as the final Ford challenger. He saved his move for the last-lap run through the frontstretch dogleg. He came up a car length short.

"When Davey and Sterling dove down to the bottom, I decided to go with them," Elliott explained. "Then Davey and Marlin got to racing among themselves, and I knew that wasn't going to get it. I just decided to go with Earnhardt."

Said Earnhardt: "I'd have to have a replay to describe it, there were so many Fords shooting at me.

"All of them seemed pretty equal. It wasn't just one. I knew I was the guy up front, and they were going to get together drafting and take a shot at passing me. I was the target."

Earnhardt said he hoped the Fords would get out of line and allow him to motor away.

"That's what Davey and Marlin did," he said. "They got down there and got to racing each other. Elliott was smart enough to get in there and push me. He knew he was going to get second place or first, and he was going to wait until the last to try."

On the final lap, Earnhardt followed the low line coming out of the fourth turn, then he moved back up in front of Elliott. Elliott tried unsuccessfully to take him on the low side.

"I knew he was going to make a move on me," said Earnhardt. "I just wasn't sure where. He stayed with me through turn three. All I could do was run her low off the corner and try to shake the air up so he wouldn't have a real good run at me.

"It was a real strategy race. He moved, I moved."

When all the scrambling was over, Mark Martin's Ford was third, Ricky Rudd's Chevy fourth and Marlin's Ford fifth. Ford drivers captured three of the top five positions, but not the one they wanted.

It was an unseasonably cool DieHard 500. Cloud cover and temperatures in the mid-80s not only set well with the fans but with the race cars. At halfway, only three cars had dropped out. Just 12 weren't around at the finish, and eight of those were benched by accidents.

The Winston 500 was over, and Davey Allison had sprayed the obligatory champagne in victory lane, and his 26-year-old wife Liz phoned the babysitter to speak to the children, Krista, 2 1/2, and Robbie, 9 months.

Krista was excited. She had watched the 500 on television, and she had a revelation for her mother: "My daddy winned the race!"

Liz, of course, knew Davey "winned" the race, but Krista saw more of it than she did. All Liz saw was the exact moment when he won.

"I was in the family paddock, standing where I could view the finish line," Liz said. "I looked out as he took the checkered flag."

She admitted that she didn't watch her 31-year-old husband's races. "I get very upset. Whether it's good or bad, I don't watch." She usually sat in a car or RV at the track and listened on the radio, but on this day she didn't even do that.

"I was particularly nervous today," she said. "I didn't really have a bad feeling—I just had a feeling. I had the same kind of feeling I had at Daytona.

"I knew he was going to run well. When he feels like he is really going to run well, that makes me nervous. I'm afraid something will happen because it has happened so many times before when he has run well."

Allison was rolling. He had won three of the nine races, was leading the points standings, had earned nearly $600,000 and was two-thirds of the way home on the Winston Million. His fans could envision him making more than $3 million. Did the Allisons dream about all the money that could land in their bank account?

"Honestly, we don't," Liz said, "and I know that's hard for people to believe. Davey would drive if they didn't pay anything and he had to get another job to make a living. Winning $2 million would not affect Davey. He's not a money person."

In the post-race interview, Davey echoed Liz: "I didn't get into racing for money. I'm fortunate that I have an opportunity to make a good living, but I still don't race for money. I race because I enjoy it."

But money provided a nice lifestyle. "We have a rather large plane that takes about $550 an hour to run," Liz

said. "And Davey has been taking helicopter lessons. He wants to buy one."

She had watched her husband score his eighth and final Talladega victory. In July of 1993 Davey was fatally injured when his helicopter crashed at Talladega Superspeedway.

The Hueytown, AL, driver won three Winston Cup races, four ARCA events and an IROC contest at Talladega.

His victory in the 1992 Winston 500 came after a typically dramatic Talladega ending. A crowd estimated at 142,500 saw him win by two car lengths, with runnerup Bill Elliott and Dale Earnhardt finishing side by side.

There was an eight-lap shoot-out after a final caution period. Allison, Elliott, Sterling Marlin, Morgan Shepherd, Earnhardt and Ernie Irvan were its lead players.

Allison was in front as the last lap began, and that's where he stayed. "We were able to hold everybody off with that 95-foot-wide Thunderbird," the driver of the Robert Yates Ford joked.

Said Allison: "I knew the Chevrolets definitely weren't going to go anywhere the Fords went. And I knew the guys back there in Fords definitely weren't going to help the Chevrolets, either. So the only thing I really had to be concerned with was where Bill went."

The challengers made their move on Allison on the front stretch.

"You never know whether somebody's saving something," Allison said. "With Bill, I didn't know if he was holding back a little and he could actually run harder. With Dale, you never know what to expect. He doesn't mind rubbing paint. We don't either.

"I think the fact Dale got alongside Bill helped us open the gap. When two cars get side by side, they slow down.

"I really don't know what would have happened if anybody else would have been in my spot. Certainly all five of those cars had shown their strength throughout the day.

"Sterling could pretty much lead at will. Dale could get through traffic as good as anybody. Once Ernie got going, he was able to run good, too. And, of course, Bill was

Davey Allison was hard to catch in the '92 Winston

(above) Alan Kulwicki (7) and Richard Petty (43) race each other in the Winston 500.
(left) Allison leads the cheerleading after a win in the 1992 Winston

Davey Allison shares the glory of victory in the Winston 500 with team owner Robert Yates, Pop Allison, Mom Allison and wife, Liz.

right there—either first, second or third all day long."

Elliott said, "I was going to try and make a move on Davey, but it just never panned out. I knew Dale wasn't going to go with me. Ernie was helping him. If Sterling could have gotten to me, he and I would've won the race.

"When Earnhardt got on the outside of me, we were all messed up."

Elliott was battling an unusual problem—a burned back.

"The first of the race went so long I thought I was going to die," he said. "I told the crew on the radio that on the first caution to have ice ready.

"I'm so tall and long-legged that they have to move the seat back for me, and it puts the seat back by the roll cage. The exhaust running under the car heats the floorboard, and the roll cage just radiates the heat on me. It was like I was sitting in a frying pan.

"I was sick at my stomach from being so hot when we finally got a caution. They had to spray me down and dump ice in my lap. They kept putting ice on my lap on every stop."

Said Earnhardt: "If I had gotten some help I believe we could have passed Davey and all of them. That's the way

it is. We were racing each other for position."

The Chevy-driving Earnhardt was cheerful after finishing third. "We ran as good as we could," he said. "It was a great race. I was like a lion in a herd of antelope out there with the Fords. They'd tolerate me as long as I didn't charge."

A $1 million bonus, the Winston Million, awaited any driver who could win three of the Big Four. Davey had nailed the Daytona 500 and the Winston 500, and he had Charlotte's Coca-Cola 600 and Darlington's Southern 500 ahead.

"Let's put it this way," said Allison, who had won the Coca-Cola 600 in 1991. "I'm leaving my favorite track to go to my second favorite track."

But, he said, he didn't like to let his thoughts settle on the Winston Million "because I think that might take away from what our real goal is. The Big Apple is what we want, and that's at the end of the season."

The Winston Cup champion is recognized at a lavish banquet in New York.

"There is another million up for grabs there, and a great big trophy, plus we get bragging rights for a year."

Allison didn't win the Winston Million or the championship, but his five victories and $1,955,628 made his last full season a great one.

Ernie Irvan's favorite song? Perhaps it's *Hail to the Chief*. Irvan performs well when presidents and vice presidents are in the audience. He won the 1992 Pepsi 400 at Daytona with George Bush in attendance, and he won the 1992 DieHard 500 after Dan Quayle had commanded the gentlemen to start their engines.

"If I had enough money I'd pay them to come to the races," the Modesto, CA, driver said.

Irvan's Kodak Film Chevrolet was as yellow as the packaging of its sponsor, so it was easy to spot on the track. And since it usually was at or near the front, identification was doubly easy.

The cars of Irvan, Sterling Marlin and Davey Allison lapped the field in one of the more humdrum races in the speedway's history. Those three were the class of the field, and Irvan's was the class of the trio.

Asked if he had the fastest car, Irvan gave a revealing answer. "We could run close to the same speed of the leaders by ourselves," he said, meaning when the others were drafting with each other.

Marlin attempted a last-lap slingshot, but few among the estimated 100,000 at the track believed he could pull it off. He couldn't. He finished on Irvan's bumper, and Allison's racer, with Bobby Hillin driving relief, was 300 yards behind Marlin's.

Irvan led 41 laps, but he didn't reach the point of the 188-lap race until the 111th lap.

Four laps into the event, one of his tires got cut, and he lost a lap. He drafted back to the front and got back into the lap with the pacesetters on the 51st circuit when they pitted and he stayed out. Leader Ricky Rudd was trying to lap him when a fan threw debris onto the track, and Irvan caught the resultant caution flag on lap 70, enabling him to catch up.

With an average speed of 176.309 miles an hour. It the fastest DieHard 500, Irvin was on a roll; he had won three of the most recent six races.

For five years, Ernie Irvan labored in the Winston Cup vineyard without a victory. Then in 1991, he won the Daytona 500 and another race, and he was enjoying a successful 1992 season.

"Larry McClure picked me to drive his car a couple of

years ago, and that took guts," Irvan said. "Larry has put together the best team in Winston Cup racing."

Irvan told his crew to keep him close on his final pit stop and he'd handle the rest. And he did, zooming back into the lead. "The car was that good all day," McClure said. "You could see that. He passed every car out there, and then he won the race.

"Ernie can win one-on-one with anybody if he's got equal equipment. He had pretty good equipment today."

Irvan became the 20th winner in 24 editions of Talladega's summer event.

It was the final Talladega appearance for Richard Petty. The retiring king of stock car racing ran 15th.

"On the plus side, I feel good about leaving here running at the finish," Petty said. "I'm glad I didn't have to get out of the car. I guess it was decent."

Much of the DieHard 500's drama centered around a driver who was in his car for just a few laps. Davey Allison started the race with two broken bones in his right arm and a broken collarbone after a terrible crash a week earlier at Pocono.

Hillin was his reliever, and when a fortuitous shower brought out a caution flag five laps into the race, the team was able to change drivers without losing a lap.

Allison was nine behind Bill Elliott in the points standings when the race began, but since the starting driver is awarded the points, Hillin's third-place finish enabled Davey to regain the lead by one over Elliott, who ran fifth.

(Alan Kulwicki would win the 1992 championship, with Elliott second and Allison third. During the 1993 season, Kulwicki and Allison would be fatally injured in separate aircraft crashes).

"I did my job," said Hillin, who led the race twice for 30 laps. "Davey is back in the points lead. It feels great."

"The Good Lord was with us," Allison said. "I would have liked to have driven a little longer because that car was just flying, but this was really a great break for the race team. I saw the raindrops, and I knew the caution was coming."

When Allison pitted, his crew removed the steering wheel, and Davey pushed himself out the window with

Rusty Wallace was the early leader in the '92 DieHard

(left) Ernie Irvan stretches his lead over Mast.
(below) Quick pit stops helped Ernie Irvan to a victory.

Irvan relaxes in victory lane.

his legs and good left arm. Hillin climbed in, buckled up and returned to the track, in the same lap with the leaders.

Allison hugged his wife Liz, ran to his race car transporter, changed into street clothes and then rode with a Talladega County deputy sheriff to a VIP suite behind the grandstand, and from that vantage point he directed Hillin by radio.

When it was over, Allison told his sub over the radio: "Bobby, that's a super job. We came out of this thing smelling like a rose. I just hope I was of some help. I want to tell you how much I appreciate everything. I hope some day we can do something for you."

"The main thing he did on the radio," Hillin explained, "was just keep telling me to calm down."

Larry McReynolds, Allison's crew chief, was delighted with the way the drama played out. "When you consider where we were seven days ago, we couldn't be happier," he said. "We got the rain, and the driver swap went well. Finishing third is the third best thing that could happen to us, but we're more than happy with that."

Hillin didn't merely motor around the track. He had a shot at winning. In fact, Allison told him on the radio from his transporter, "We've got a good car. Everything

feels good. We can win with it."

A slow pit stop under green on lap 171 knocked him out of the front draft, though, and ended his chance at victory.

"I just couldn't get out of the pits fast enough on the last stop," Hillin said. "I saw Sterling Marlin leaving the pits, and I was sure he was speeding, but I guess he wasn't. I slowed down a little to keep from getting penalized. That was enough to keep me out of contention for the win."

The strategy was never to stroke, McReynolds said. "It would have been real easy to tell Bobby to take it easy, to sit back in the pack, bring home a top-10 finish and pack it up and take it home. But our game plan was the same it has been every race since the first one at Daytona, and that's try to win."

Elliott shrugged off his loss of the lead in points standings. "I ain't worried about it. They got a break, and they're back in front in the points race. But there's a lot of racing left.

"This car never got going today. What a piece of junk."

Rusty Wallace had been standing the Winston Cup circuit on its ear, but his car got stood on its nose at the finish of a wild Winston 500 before an estimated 145,000 fans.

The St. Louis driver had won three races in a row and four of the eight that had been contested in 1993. If he could win at Talladega he would share the modern record of four straight victories. Cale Yarborough accomplished the feat in 1976, Darrell Waltrip in 1981, Dale Earnhardt in 1987, Harry Gant in 1991 and Bill Elliott in 1992.

Wallace wasn't making any boastful predictions, though. The 2.66-mile Talladega Superspeedway had never been good to him. "I'd like to get a top-five and get out of here," he admitted before the race.

But Rusty had owned April, visiting victory lane after every event contested during the month. He had won at Bristol, North Wilkesboro and Martinsville. All, of course, are short tracks, but Wallace had demonstrated his superspeedway prowess, too, by taking Atlanta in March.

After just eight races, Wallace had single-handedly given Pontiac more victories than the marquee enjoyed in all of 1992 when it won three.

"The Pontiac body is 8 or 10 percent better," Wallace reflected before the Winston 500. "Our engine program is a ton better. We've got a better chassis. I'm a better driver. I think clearer in the car. We get good pit stops."

The man who won just once in 1992 smiled grimly and added, "And I'm just darn tired of getting my butt kicked."

Waltrip compared Wallace's streak to Elliott's four-win string of the year before. "Bill won some races that you could say he shouldn't have won—but there's none Rusty shouldn't have won. In fact, you could say he should have won the Daytona 500, too."

Wallace was indeed a strong entry in the sport's Super Bowl, but an end-over-end, barrel-rolling crash that made all the video highlights eliminated him from the Daytona field. He had run as high as third and challenged for second before he became the innocent victim of a skirmish between two other drivers.

His Daytona crash was so spectacular that it was featured on the "How'd They Do That?" TV show, which explained how NASCAR's rollbars protect drivers—those

same rollbars that would save Rusty's life at Talladega.

Just what was the edge that Wallace enjoyed as he compiled his early-1993 streak, someone asked Dale Jarrett, winner of that Daytona 500?

"Not to be a smart aleck," Jarrett replied, "but if we knew the edge we'd be catching up to him."

But the other side of the coin—and this obviously weighed heavily on Wallace's mind—was his poor record over the years at the circuit's fastest track, Talladega Superspeedway.

In 18 races, his average finish had been 17.6. He had never finished higher than fifth, and he had a couple of 37ths, a 35th and a 32nd. Indeed, he failed to qualify on the first day of time trials for the 1993 Winston 500 and started 24th.

Before the race someone asked him why Talladega had been so vexing for him.

"I don't know," Wallace replied. "If I knew the reason, we'd fix it."

But then he elaborated: "We have never really hit on how to get a car to go fast around Talladega." He and his men could make one handle at the monster track, but there were times his racers "felt like they had a parachute tied behind them."

So Wallace shook his head when newsmen called him the favorite and repeated that he'd love to know he could get fifth place.

What he got was sixth place, a car that looked as if it had fallen off the Empire State Building, a broken wrist and a concussion.

Ernie Irvan won the race with a last-lap charge that nipped Jimmy Spencer. Earnhardt's car tagged Wallace's, and Rusty's machine flipped 10 times, end over end, side over side. It was airborne when it crossed the finish line.

Wallace was airlifted to Carraway Methodist Medical Center in Birmingham. He was kept in the hospital for two nights and released, and he drove the next event at Sonoma, two weeks later, without relief.

Wallace was leading the Winston 500 when rain began to fall and the caution flag appeared with eight laps to go. Earnhardt shot by him on the backstretch and led as the cars crossed the finish line. If the event continued until

The 1993 Winston 500 was the second in a row for Irvan at Talladega.

Dale Jarrett gets by (1) Rick Mast, (41) Phil Parsons and (28) Davey Allison on his way to a third place finish.

Four-wide racing in the trioval during the Winston 500.

Bumper to bumper driving in front of the grandstand.

the end under yellow, Earnhardt would be the winner.

But with four laps to go, NASCAR waved the red flag, stopping the cars. There were three hours of daylight remaining, the sanctioning body reminded. It would fold its hands and wait for the rain to stop.

The announcement sent thousands of fans to their cars and onto the highways. They would beat the traffic and listen to the ending on their radios, the escapees reasoned.

Big mistake. They missed one of the most incredible finishes in the history of stock car racing.

The rain delay lasted just 14 minutes. The engines were fired, two laps were run under yellow, and then the green signaled a two-lap banzai dash to the end.

Before the rain, Earnhardt and Wallace had appeared too strong for the others. Indeed, on the green restart, they began pulling away, but Irvan and Spencer surged by Dale and Rusty, Irvan winning and Stricklin finishing second.

It was the third-straight Talladega victory for the Modesto, CA, driver. Irvan won a Grand National event on the day before he took the 1992 DieHard 500.

But Wallace's wreck commanded most of the crowd's attention at the end.

When the car stopped rolling the sheet metal had been

distributed over the premises, and the carcass that remained consisted of frame, engine and rollbars.

For 15 minutes after the race, fans waited in their seats, radios to their ears, to learn Wallace's fate. They feared the worst. Then suddenly it was obvious the news had come, for they cheered in chorus and headed for the exits. Wallace's injuries didn't match the ferocity of the crash.

The man once deprecatingly called Swervin' Irvan because of his unpredictable driving said he played it cool.

"Lots of times today I had shots that I could have dived in there three-wide and four-wide," Irvan, a man with the doleful eyes of a basset hound, said, "but my experience told me not to. I didn't make moves that I used to would have made."

The driver of the Morgan-McClure Chevrolet feared his bid for victory might be eclipsed at the end, but it didn't happen. "I thought, 'Here comes Spencer, trying to win his first race, and where does that usually happen? At Talladega.'"

1993

A quarter-century of action at Talladega Superspeedway ended with a moment that was a microcosm of racing at the world's most competitive track.

Dale Earnhardt and Ernie Irvan finished the DieHard 500 side by side. Earnhardt's official margin of victory: six inches.

With 12 laps to go, Kyle Petty led a six-car string that drafted clear of the field. With three laps remaining, Earnhardt, Irvan and Dale Jarrett surged by Petty. Then it was Earnhardt and Irvan, door to door, around the final circuit. Mark Martin, Petty, Jarrett and Greg Sacks followed Irvan in the finish order.

"I just out-dueled them," Earnhardt said of the closing laps. "I didn't think I had them until we beat them to the line. They'd move, we'd move. One would drag by you, you'd pass them back. It was just an all-day game. We made the last move, and it worked.

"All of them were players, and all of them were important. You didn't know who was going to push whom, who was going to help whom or who was going to hurt whom. I just had to play my hand. You had to play the game until the last move, and we got the last move. It was one of those see-saw deals, and I was on the last saw."

Said Irvan: "Dale and I had a heck of a drag race coming to the finish. I've won a few on the last lap. You've got to take the bad with the good."

It was Earnhardt's eighth victory in various types of racing at Talladega—tying the Mooresville, NC, driver with Davey Allison as the track's winningest driver.

Allison, a 32-year-old father of two, suffered fatal injuries when the helicopter he was piloting crashed in the speedway's infield on July 12. Driver Red Farmer, his Hueytown, AL, friend and neighbor, was the only passenger. Farmer was injured but was released from the hospital two days later.

Two other Hueytown residents, Neil and David Bonnett had gone to the track to test David's Grand National car. Allison and Farmer were eating lunch at the Iceberg, a Hueytown cafe that is popular with the racing set, when Allison suggested they fly to Talladega in his helicopter to be with the Bonnetts.

During the landing procedure, the craft was near the ground when it suddenly shot up, gyrated, and fell back to earth, Farmer said.

They were rushed by helicopter to Carraway Methodist Medical Center in Birmingham, where Allison died of head injuries the next morning.

It was the latest in an incredible series of tragedies that struck Bobby Allison and his wife Judy. Bobby was grievously injured in a crash at Pocono in 1988, and since then has raced only in an exhibition. Their son Clifford was killed when his car crashed at Michigan during practice, 11 months before the accident that took Davey's life. Davey was injured several times in wrecks in 1992, once in a spectacular series of flips at Pocono.

In a touching ceremony before the DieHard 500, Allison's widow Liz thanked the fans for their support, and his uncle Donnie drove his No. 28 racer around the track.

Robby Gordon, a 24-year-old Indianapolis car driver who had never been to Talladega, was the surprise choice to replace Allison in Robert Yates' racer for the DieHard 500. Much of the fan support for Allison was transferred to Gordon, but his unfamiliarity with driving stocks on the big speedway was evident when his car spun without being touched by another and hit the wall. He got last place.

The 25th DieHard 500 was a wild race that seared fans' emotions, already rubbed raw by the death of Allison.

A five-car crash on lap 70 left another Alabama driver, Stanley Smith of Chelsea, in very critical condition with a head injury. He, too, was helicoptered to Carraway. Smith, an occasional Winston Cup competitor, was making his first start of the season. He survived.

A crowd estimated at 95,000 saw that crash send Jimmy Horton's car over the concrete guardrail in the first turn. It plunged down the four-story embankment outside the speedway, tore through a fence and came to rest on its wheels, the remains barely resembling an automobile. Horton—who thus became the only driver ever to sail outside Talladega's racing area—wasn't seriously injured.

"I like dirt racing, but not that much," quipped

Neil Bonnett raced at Talladega for the first time since 1989.

Traffic was heavy all day during the 1993 DieHard 500.

Earnhardt moves around traffic on the outside.

Childress and Earnhardt display their marble winner's trophies.

Horton, who was covered with red dirt from his excursion down the earthen bank. "There was dirt flying all around, and once I saw the dirt I knew I was in trouble. I looked at the car as I was getting out, and it's pretty much of a mess. These cars are built safe, and that's why we get in. We'll go racing again."

Neil Bonnett was making his first start since he was seriously injured in a crash in 1990. He drove a Chevrolet owned by Richard Childress as a teammate to his friend Earnhardt.

On lap 131, Bonnett got caught in a multi-car accident. Upside down, his car flew over one driven by Ted Musgrave. It hit the heavily cabled catch fence on the frontstretch, and the race was stopped for 70 minutes while the fence was repaired.

Bonnett's flight was caught on the CBS-TV camera inside his car, and television watchers got a unique view of a startling crash.

"I knew it was upside down, and I felt a real hard lick," Bonnett said. "I couldn't tell what it was. I'm not hurt at all. I've just got a bruise on the back of my arm. Richard Childress' team not only builds fast race cars, they build safe ones, too."

Despite the violent ending of his racing day, Bonnett was upbeat about his return to competition.

"Let me tell you, I've never felt this good going into a race," he said. "I was working in this direction the last few months. I felt good out there. I mean, I really wasn't running the car like the thing needs to go. I was trying to use my head all day and stay in the right place.

"I hate for something like that to happen, but I'm telling you, there's not a guy on that race track that doesn't try anything but to go to the front. Stuff like that is going to happen."

With one car destroyed and another in victory lane, team owner Childress had experienced quite a day. "I'm glad Neil is okay, and I've got all the confidence in the world in Dale on the last lap," he said. "We've lost a few like we won today, but we've won our share of close ones, too."

Earnhardt not only won the DieHard 500, he authored an historical footnote. There were 26 lead changes among 10 drivers, the 16th coming when he passed Jeff Gordon on lap 106. That was the 1,000th lead change in the DieHard 500, which is the only Winston Cup track to reach that figure.

One of the early motorcycle races at Talladega in 1971.

It was almost as if Clark Kent had ducked into a phone booth the day Bill Ward ducked into victory lane at Talladega. Ward wasn't a mild-mannered reporter; he was a mild-mannered insurance agent in nearby Anniston, AL. Yet, there he was, accepting the victor's plaudits at the biggest, fastest track in the world.

Ward won the 1970 Bama 200, a Saturday preliminary to the Talladega 500. A newspaper story appropriately compared him to Walter Mitty, for the 40-year-old Ward was only marginally a race driver.

He had driven dirt-trackers and sports cars and midgets on a few occasions but, as he put it after the Bama 200: "Racing is just a hobby to me. I'm not serious about it, and I don't plan to go into it. I'm a State Farm agent in Anniston. I insure safe drivers."

Ward's name was linked to the speedway, though. Not because he was a racer, but because he was the man who, at the request of Bill France, had located the land on which it eventually was built.

His winning a race there was a strange turn of events at a track that would become synonymous with unpredictability.

Ward's first start on a superspeedway was in the 1969

Bama 400, a Grand Touring race that was contested the day before the 1969 Talladega 500. In that event, Ken Rush of High Point, NC, made history by becoming the first winner at the track. Ward finished ninth.

Ward, now 63 and still selling insurance in Anniston, smiled at the recollection. "Basically, I told France, 'If you're going to build that track, I want to race on it.'"

T.C. Hunt brought his backup Camaro for Ward to drive in the 400. It wasn't planned, but when leading drivers boycotted the Talladega 500, Ward drove in it too, finishing 11th.

"We didn't have but one set of tires, and we ran them both days," he said. "Of course, those little cars didn't wear out tires. We had to stay down out of the way in the 500 or we would have gotten run over."

Tom Pistone provided Ward with a Mustang for the 1970 Bama 200 GT event. "I beat David Pearson out of the pole and won the race," Ward said. "It was a dream come true. It was weird. Today, somebody like me couldn't even get in a race.

"The oil cooler exploded near the end and blew hot oil on my legs, and I had to wear bedroom slippers for a week. The last 10 laps I didn't know what was going on. I

Bill France Sr., and Bill France Jr., at a 1969 IMSA race at the track.

couldn't have gone many more laps because oil was pumping out in the car and puddling up.

"David Pearson came over and said, 'Ward, you've got to be crazy. I wouldn't have driven that car for anything.'

"But winning that race helped me a lot. I got a lot of good publicity out of it. And it opened a lot of doors for me in racing."

Bitten by the superspeedway racing bug, Ward graduated to Winston Cup, driving only at Talladega. He was in every Winston Cup race there through 1975. "I'd run ARCA on Saturday and Winston Cup on Sunday," he said. "I never did have any good cars, though."

Given his ties to the speedway, it is strange to hear Ward say, "I haven't been back to the Talladega track since I climbed out of my car in August of 1975."

Tiny Lund was killed in the 1975 Talladega 500. "My wife Claudette was standing there when they brought Tiny in," Ward said. "I later had to go to the hospital for heat exhaustion. My family retired me then.

"If I couldn't drive race cars, I didn't want to be around race cars."

Talladega Superspeedway is world famous as the scene of the most competitive events on the Winston Cup circuit, but over its first 25 years it hosted races of various types.

Motorcycles, sports cars, International Race of Champions cars, Automobile Racing Club of America stocks, Busch Grand National stocks, open-cockpit Formula Vees and Formula Fords and other machines raced there. Some of the races were preliminaries to the

> *Talladega is world famous as the scene of the most competitive events on the Winston Cup circuit, but over its first 25 years it hosted races of various types.*

WC main events and some stood alone.

As the first quarter century ended, the speedway had settled into a routine of two race weeks a year. An event in the International Race of Champions series and an ARCA contest were the preliminaries on the day before the Winston 500, and a Busch race was the preliminary on the day before the DieHard 500.

The first motorcycle meet, in 1970, featured the Talladega 200. Twenty-year-old Dave Aldana was the winner on a BSA.

The track not only was fast for cars but for cycles. Aldana's average of 104.589 miles an hour on the four-mile course that combined the stock car track and an infield road was the fastest ever in the U.S. The race pulled an estimated 12,500 fans.

Various types of sports car races were run, employing everything from powerful, exotic machines to small sedans but, like the motorcycles, sports cars didn't have sufficient drawing power in Alabama—stock car country—and they were dropped from the schedule.

An event that was interesting in its conception was the Bama 200 of 1972. It included a mixed field of NASCAR pony cars and International Motor Sports Association sports cars.

The NASCAR machines were given a one-minute head start. Though it was actually two races in one, the drama was in watching the IMSA cars try to catch up. Wilbur Pickett and Tony DeLorenzo gave IMSA the first two places, in Corvettes. NASCAR's Tiny Lund was third in a Firebird. Pickett and Lund each received first-place money. The race drew an estimated 12,500 fans.

In October of 1969, the month after the first Talladega 500, the track hosted a 300-mile Sportsman race on Saturday and a 500-mile ARCA race on Sunday. Lund won the Permatex 300 and Jim Vandiver the Vulcan 500.

Davey Allison's red and gold car (23) prepares for his first race at Talladega in the 1982 ARCA 200.

Neither drew a large crowd.

ARCA events became the staple in the preliminary role at Talladega, with the Busch racers not showing there until 1992, and the driver who was most responsible for the Saturday ARCA crowds rising into the 40,000 range was Davey Allison.

The son of the great Bobby Allison, the youngster from nearby Hueytown, AL, built the foundation of the Winston Cup career that was to follow on ARCA victories at Talladega.

His first one came in the spring of 1983, and he said,

"This was the biggest race I've won, probably the most important in my career." He swept both Talladega ARCA events that year and won one in 1984 and another in 1985 for a total of four.

But the winningest ARCA driver at Talladega was Grant Adcox, an affable Chattanoogan who won both races in 1986 and both in 1987 before Red Farmer snapped his four-victory string in the spring of 1988. Adcox won again in the summer of 1988 for five Talladega ARCA triumphs.

IROC, which matches world-class drivers from various

Road racers mix it up on the infield course.

segments of racing in equally prepared cars, made a rousing debut in 1984 when Darrell Waltrip beat Cale Yarborough by eight inches. Yarborough won in 1986, Dale Earnhardt in 1990, Rusty Wallace in 1991, and Davey Allison in 1992 before Indy-car racing's Al Unser Jr. broke up the stock car monopoly in 1993.

The Busch series supplanted ARCA as the preliminary fare before the DieHard 500 in 1992, with Ernie Irvan winning before an estimated 45,000. Earnhardt won the 1993 Busch race.

For a while, setting world's closed-course speed records at Talladega was popular. A.J. Foyt did 217.85 miles an hour in an Indy car in 1974. Mark Donohue broke the record by reaching 221.120 in a Can-Am Porsche in 1975. But by 1986, Indy cars were running faster than Donohue's in qualifying at Michigan.